JOURNEY *to* EXCELLENCE

The Young Golfer's Complete Guide to
Achievement and Personal Growth

HENRY BRUNTON
with MICHAEL GRANGE

First Printing July 2009

Sea Script Company

Seattle, Washington

ISBN: 978-0-615-30293-5

Library of Congress Card Catalogue No.: 2009930884

Cover design by David Marty

Text layout by Colleen Edwards

Cover photo by Chris Gallow

www.gallowstudios.com

SEA   SCRIPT   COMPANY
www.seascriptcompany.com
info@seascriptcompany.com
206.748.0345

CONTENTS

FOREWORD

by Johnny Miller

I SPEND A LOT OF MY TIME watching the best golfers in the
world do what they do best. And I love what I do. It's a privilege
watching Tiger or Phil or any of the other stars on the PGA Tour
or LPGA Tour golf their ball. But that doesn't mean I haven't left
my heart in San Francisco. It's the city I grew up in and where I
started my wonderful journey through golf.

It was my dad who started me in the game with a couple of
sawed off wooden clubs. There were a lot of good public courses
in San Francisco in the those days, and a lot of really good golfers
came from the city—Ken Venturi, George Archer, Bob Rosburg—
just to name the major champions. I used to play at Harding and
Lincoln Park, a hilly muni with tiny greens. I hit it so short I could
barely get up one side of the hills and down the next. But I loved to
figure how to make the ball go where I wanted off all the strange
lies you would get there.

In the winters my Dad would set up a canvas tarp in the ceiling
of our basement and I would whack balls in there for hours.
Because I couldn't see the ball's flight, I got good at identifying
a good strike by the sound and feel. I loved hearing that crisp
thwack at impact and even from the TV booth, I can usually tell

immediately if an iron shot is mis-hit and if it will come up short or not have enough spin to hold.

You hear stories about kids being pressured to excel in golf, which makes no sense. Golf should be a pleasure, and the preparation you need to do to play your best should be a pleasure too. You can learn about yourself in competition and realize the discipline it takes to reach your potential and the maturity it takes to handle disappointments and triumphs with grace and class, but playing should be fun above all. I saw how the fun got sucked out of it for some kids when my four sons were playing junior golf, and never liked it.

I was very lucky because my father was always positive and never pushed. He always called me Champ. Playing on the PGA Tour and winning the U.S. Open and British Open were huge thrills, but some of my most exciting moments in the game came well before that. I was lucky enough to become the first invited junior member at the Olympic Club in San Francisco. I was 14 and all I kept hearing was how the U.S. Open was coming in a few years. I knew for sure I was going to caddie at it, but I kept working on my game and was able to qualify to compete as a 19-year-old amateur. I finished tied for eighth at the U.S. Open on my home course. It was a dream come true and a big step along the way in my personal journey to excellence. I hope you continue on your journey with golf and that you give this game a chance to make your dreams come true too. And don't ever stop having fun along the way, Champ.

—Johnny Miller

Acknowledgements

It is exciting to introduce *Journey to Excellence* to the golf world. I am grateful for the efforts and support of the many individuals and organizations that have helped make this book a reality. Thank you to all.

To my dear wife Rhonda and to Cole, the best little man anyone could have. Thanks for the encouragement, understanding, sacrifices and love.

To my publishing team: Lorin Anderson is a golf industry leader. His belief in this project and his quarterbacking skills to bring the 'team' together and make it happen are highly appreciated. Thanks to Michael Grange, heralded sports journalist at the *Toronto Globe and Mail*, for his outstanding writing and ability to convey the message just as I wanted. Thanks to Marilyn Allen, book agent extraordinaire, for the patience and sage advice needed as we navigated through the complicated modern publishing world during a time of economic turmoil. And thanks to Beth Farrell from Sea Script Company, you put the icing on the cake.

To Johnny Miller, what a thrill for me to have my boyhood idol offer assistance with the foreword. And to Pia Nilsson and Lynn Marriott, the two people who have influenced modern golf coaching the most; you have had a tremendous impact on me.

This book is a result of a lot of support from a lot of people over many, many years. Thanks to Paul Sherratt, a great friend and one of the best PGA Professionals ever anywhere. I won the lottery when I got the opportunity to be his apprentice and to be mentored by him. To Bruce Murray and Bob Hogarth, excellent Head Professionals both, working for you at Royal Montreal Golf Club provided me with great training and opportunities.

Thanks to the Governors and Executive Committee at the Royal Canadian Golf Association (RCGA). Being able to work for the RCGA as the National Men's Coach is a privilege and an honor. To CEO Scott Simmons and Chief Sport Officer Jeff Thompson, thanks for your confidence in my abilities. To Derek Ingram, my Assistant Coach, you are a terrific partner. And especially to Doug Roxburgh, Director of High Performance Programs, you are a great friend, teacher and mentor.

I am a proud Member of the Canadian PGA. I am grateful to the Association for having the opportunity to create and implement the Teaching and Coaching Certification Program (TCCP). To the Board, CEO Steve Carroll, and Director of Education Gary Bernard, thanks for your support and the opportunities you've allowed me to pursue.

The Acushnet Company has long been the golf professional's most loyal partner. I'm fortunate to be part of their extended family. The resources, training, and partnership support that I receive from them are incredible. Special thank you to Canadian President Ted Manning, Worldwide Vice-President Peter Broome, Director of Player Promotion Jim Ahern, and all of the Sales Reps throughout the organization who go above and beyond to support my efforts.

Having the optimal learning environment is paramount for effective golf coaching. Eagles Nest Golf Club and its ownership group and leaders Executive Director Duane Aubie and Director of Golf Jamie Trenholme provide me and my staff with a home base that is just that and more. It's much appreciated.

To the Caribbean Golf Association (CGA) and especially the Trinidad and Tobago Golf Association (TTGA) for opportunities to impact your junior programs and coaching. Thanks to CGA President Ash Ali; past presidents Ambrose Gouthro from Bahamas and Sidney Wolf from Puerto Rico; and all of the member country officials, as well as to TTGA President and Junior Leader Robert Costelloe for his passion, vision and friendship.

To my 'team' at Henry Brunton Golf: Jon Roy, Jeff Overholt, Patrick O'Neill, Scott Broman, Kyle Brenn, Aileen Robertson and Rhonda Fleury. Your commitment and professionalism is outstanding. Thanks for making me better and our services first class. I'm very proud of each of you.

To the club members at Rideau View Golf Club, Royal Montreal Golf Club and Emerald Hills Golf Club, thanks for the encouragement and patronage.

To the many friends and colleagues who graciously share their work and expertise: Dr. John Marshall, Peter Sanders, Dr. Deborah Graham and Jon Stabler, Dr. Rick Jensen, Dr. Gary Wiren, Fred Shoemaker, Steve Ball, Dr. Paul Schempp, Don Kotnick, Todd Sones, Bob Vokey, Dr. Bob Christina, Dr. Greg Wells, Dr. Dana Sinclair, Jack Sims, Charlie King, Dave Phillips, Greg Rose, Joanne Flynn, Dr. Jean Cote, Bob Skura, Willard Ellis, Liz Hoffman, Herb Page, Dr. Tim Lee, Dr. Steve Norris, Dr. Anders Ericsson, Greg Redman, Chad Cole, Steve Ducat,

Larry Dunn, Laird White and Michael Milligan. Thanks to all of you for your generous assistance.

To all of my junior students and their parents: Thank you for your trust and the opportunity to help you reach your goals.

INTRODUCTION

THE SINGULAR PURPOSE of publishing *Journey to Excellence* is
to positively impact aspiring young golfers and the individuals who
support their efforts—parents, coaches, volunteers and program
administrators. I hope that this book makes the game more fun
and rewarding for everyone who reads it. If it inspires people to
play more golf, encourages them to introduce others to the game
and leads them to enjoy the sport to the fullest throughout their
lives, then this project will have been a success.

I want all young golfers to enjoy golf on their own terms,
and discover and benefit from all that the sport and the people
in it offer. As well, it is my intention to arm those who have the
dream of competing at the highest levels with the knowledge,
facts and wherewithal to formulate and execute a sound player
development strategy that leads them toward their goals on and
off the course.

It's time to begin your journey to excellence—play well and
have fun!

—Henry Brunton

FOR MOM AND DAD
YOU'RE THE BEST!

1

HAVING FUN MOVING THAT WHITE BALL FROM HERE TO THERE

IN THE BEGINNING IT'S ABOUT FUN. It's about going to a golf course or a practice range or a putting green with your dad or your grandmother or an older brother, a friend or your gym class. Someone puts a club into your hands and you try to hit the white ball from here to there. What could be simpler? What could be more basic? For some reason, some people—a lot of people— have fun trying to move that white ball. There are a lot of things about it that make it fun: the company is almost always good—no one is introduced to golf by people they don't like or don't like them; it's always a gift that friends and loved ones share with each other. And rare is the person that doesn't get some simple pleasure from being outside with their feet on the grass and the warm sun on their neck. And while so many things—fun things—are about going faster and getting louder, things slow down at a golf course. People are pleased to be there and are in no rush to leave. It's a nice place to be.

But at the heart of it all is the strangely compelling allure of making that ball go from here to there. At first just moving it is a small triumph. Then the goal is to make if fly high, then far. Eventually the hope is to make it go more or less straight. The lucky few who become golfers—not just guys who play golf—they can get to the point where they can make the ball turn left or right depending on the situation. They have high shots and low shots, cuts and hooks. And they can get it in the hole, which is the point. For them playing is fun—it has to be fun or why do it—but they find something more in the game. It offers a challenge. For them the fun is not just moving that ball, it's moving the ball how they want when they want. It's putting yourself in situations where you have to make a shot at a certain moment. It's about competition. It's about learning how good you can be by finding your limits and exceeding them.

Golfers—serious golfers—are dreamers, in the best sense of the word. Golf gives them a way to make their dreams take shape. From Jack Nicklaus to Tiger Woods and Nancy Lopez to Annika Sorenstam, golf has been sustained by the young imaginations that fall in love with the sense of power and control that comes from a solidly struck shot. It makes them want to do it again and again and again, until the sun finally sets. And then they're back the next morning feeding their newfound passion.

Golf is meant to be fun, a time for friendships, laughs, disappointments and glory. But for people who get bitten by the bug, the game means a little more. They practice a little longer, watch the big tournaments with more interest and immerse themselves in the nuances, subtleties and disciplines of a game that dates back centuries, but has yet to be mastered.

They don't want to idolize their heroes on the PGA or LPGA Tours; they want to become one of them. Golf is what they dream about at night, and think about all day, the anvil on which they fashion their childhood and adolescence. It shapes who they are and the adults they become.

The question is how to make those dreams come true. Certainly hard work is essential, as golf is a game that responds to diligence. And passion is essential, as golf will test the affections of even the most enthusiastic. And talent—honed through effort and lifted by passion—is necessary too. But how does a youngster harness all of these ingredients? How does he or she find a reliable route from long summer days spent scuffing the dirt at the practice range to being the absolute best golfer they can be? And what lessons can the pursuit of excellence in golf provide young people about being the best person they can be?

This book will help young golfers and their parents answer those questions. If the goal of golf is to move that white ball from here to there, the goal of this book is help you learn how to move your game from here—as a young, promising and passionate player—to there, that place where promise and passion have been harnessed to inspire growth, development and results. Used properly, this can be a handbook, a step-by-step path by which those who have the will can find the way to reach their goals in golf and life.

Perhaps the first thing you'll notice is what isn't in this book: There are no elaborate swing sequences or complicated drawings showing just the right way to start your take away or how to hit your driver 10 yards farther. This isn't to say that mechanics aren't an important part of the game. But there are plenty of places to get that information. Ideally you're getting it from a qualified and competent coach. The goal here is to help you know what to look for when you're trying to find that coach. Becoming the best golfer you can be involves much more than swing mechanics. It involves thinking big while at the same time paying attention to the small details that allow big things to happen.

Grand dreams precede great accomplishments. But in reality, dreams of a career in professional golf are just that. Even playing college golf at a high level is something to which many junior golfers aspire, though few ever reach. But it's a worthy pursuit if undertaken wisely. The lessons learned in trying to maximize your golf potential are applicable across any number of disciplines: time management, goal setting, dealing with success and failure and grace under pressure. The young golfer who masters these will not only become the best golfer they can be, but the best person.

The best place to start is at the beginning and with some facts. Did you know that there are 2.2 million junior aged golfers in the United States? Did you know there are less than 500 men and women on the PGA Tour and LPGA Tours combined? And that those lucky few come from all over the world? When it comes to making it big in golf, the math is not encouraging. We dream when we're asleep, but for dreams to have a good chance of becoming reality, it's important to have your eyes wide open. It's important to dream big and set your goals high. But it's important to know that making it a personal goal to play on the PGA Tour or LPGA Tour or even NCAA Division I golf is a very small step in the process. If you use the faraway goal of playing elite competitive golf as a way to develop consistent and useful practice habits and learn how to manage your time and bring similar discipline to other parts of your life, you will be a success in golf and in other parts of your life even if the closest you ever get to professional golf is watching it on television.

And if you think reaching those goals is something you can do yourself without help, well, congratulations. Your sense of independence is to be admired. But the reality is it takes a village to raise a successful golfer, from parents willing to invest the time, money and energy to allow you to pursue your passion to friends and competitors to push you. Vital to the process is finding and working with the right coach, someone who can help you identify your goals and establish a long-term strategy to help you meet them.

That strategy has to be multifaceted. As you progress in the sport, you will need to become an expert in what role equipment has in your play as you enter the world of custom-fitted clubs and balls that match your swing and club characteristics. Obviously becoming a top-flight golfer requires practice. No one could think otherwise, could they? But do people think carefully enough about practice? Or is it something you do for a couple of hours a few days a week during golf season? Because the reality is practice is like oxygen to a serious golfer. It needs careful attention and planning. Proper practice habits need to be taught, learned and improved on over time. And that's just the physical side of the game.

Elite golf requires as much of you mentally as physically. To be a champion, or even to reach your potential, you need to think like a champion. Again, this sounds like a cliché, but it's far from it. You can improve your mental approach every bit as much as you can improve your short game or wedge play. It can be argued that you can't really improve your short game or wedge play *until* you improve your mental approach. There are lessons to be learned here too. Just as there are lessons to be learned about how to improve your golf-related fitness and nutrition habits; how to manage your time and plan your season to maximize your opportunity to succeed—everything from learning how to set practical goals to periodization to budgeting. Ultimately all of this hard work may put you in position to seriously consider playing golf at the college level and maybe even beyond that. But that takes some thought and planning as well, from determining what you want to get out of the college experience academically to finding a golf program that fits your personal, golf and academic needs.

Playing golf at college or even professionally is a long way from that moment when someone handed you a club and you tried to move the little white ball from here to there. But in a way it's no distance at all. Why did you want to move that white ball? Because it was there. Why did you want to do it again? Because you wanted to do it better. And the better you did it, the more you wanted to do it, and the more you wanted to do it, the better you wanted to get. The journey never changes, but the farther you go, the more important it is to know the right steps to take. It's what keeps it fun.

2

MANY ARE CALLED, FEW ARE CHOSEN: THE FACTS ABOUT ELITE GOLF

FROM A DISTANCE, say the 10 feet between you and the television set, professional golf looks pretty good. Easy, even. The courses look lush, tee shots find the fairways, approaches find the greens and putts find the hole. Which is why, on the major professional golf tours, an even par score on a course that measures well over 7,000 yards is just good enough to get you beat.

Consider the case of Victor Ciesielski. The strapping 6-foot-4, 210 pounder from Cambridge, Ontario had the ride of his life at the 2006 Canadian Open held at Hamilton Golf and Country Club. A late-blooming amateur playing out of nearby Galt Country Club, Ciesielski was enjoying a pretty good summer. By his own estimation, he had played his last 40 rounds at even-par or better. He won his club championship and shot a 61, breaking PGA Tour pro Ian Leggatt's course record. Things got even better when he teed it up in a Monday final qualifying event. There were four spots available in the field for the Open, and Ciesielski got into the tournament by firing a five-under-par round of 66 to earn his way into his national championship.

Ciesielski didn't stop there. In his opening round, he shot 68 and was low Canadian heading into the second round where he shot 70—including an ace—to qualify for the weekend, becoming only the third amateur to manage that in the past 20 years. "I'm missing frosh week at school right now, but I can't imagine it being any more fun than this," said Ciesielski, who is enrolled at the University of Waterloo. "It's amazing. It's just a dream come true."

Reality set in sooner than he would have hoped. He shot a 77 in his final round, and left the golf course mystified. How could that have happened? The difference between his first round and his last wasn't particularly obvious. There were some more putts missed, and a few more fairways too. But he wasn't rifling balls out of bounds. His worst score on any given hole was a double-bogey. But still. Double hockey sticks. And just like that Cinderella was a chambermaid again. But there's hope for Ciesielski. Not only is he talented, he's smart too. Consider his reaction to his final round boo-boo. He'd just played some of the best golf of his life, and faced the harsh reality that it wasn't good enough. "I learned a lot," he said of his week on the PGA Tour. "How to handle the media, how to carry yourself, what it's like out here and what it takes to make a living. Four-over-par just doesn't cut it. It doesn't matter if you make the cut, you can't scrape from the bottom of the barrel. You've got to be on the top of your game, and I wasn't.

"It's a very eye-opening experience. Even though I played pretty well and everyone thinks I played well, it's not even close to where I need to be. Everyone is really consistent. Like I might have strung a couple good rounds together, but when these guys shoot the same as me, it's probably not a good round for them. They probably have a lot of stuff that just went wrong out there. Well, things were clicking for me. So I need to take a couple more steps forward instead of this one today backwards."

PRO GOLF DREAMS

SETTING YOUR GOALS HIGH IS A PROVEN PATH TO SUCCESS. AFTER ALL, IF YOU REACH FOR THE STARS, YOU MIGHT JUST GRAB THE MOON. BUT IF YOUR GOAL IS TO PLAY ON THE PGA TOUR, YOU'RE SETTING YOUR GOALS VERY HIGH INDEED. HOW HIGH? PRO GOLF DREAMS, BY THE NUMBERS:

2.2 MILLION: THE NUMBER OF JUNIOR GOLFERS ACTIVE IN THE UNITED STATES
226,000: JUNIORS PLAYING COMPETITIVE GOLF
5,500: GOLFERS PLAYING AT THE NCAA DIVISION I LEVEL
446: MEN AND WOMEN PLAYING ON THE PGA TOUR AND LPGA TOUR COMBINED

Ciesielski is lucky. He got his exposure to big-time golf early on, and will be able to take those lessons back to the practice green and driving range. It's worth considering how hard some of those lessons can be.

In 2001 a young golfer named Ty Tryon began making waves on the PGA Tour. A protégé of David Leadbetter's, who has worked with everyone from the Big Easy (Ernie Els) to the Big Wiesy (Michelle Wie), Tryon became the youngest golfer since 1957 to make the cut on the PGA Tour when he fired rounds of 67 and 73 to qualify for weekend play at the Honda Classic. He eventually finished tied for 39th. Later that same season, he tied 37th at the BC Open. And then he went better, as he lasted through the PGA Tour's gruelling qualifying tournament and became the youngest golfer to ever earn his PGA Tour card, in part by firing a final round of 66.

But things have never worked out exactly the way they were planned since then. Tryon played only five events as a rookie before missing the rest of the season with mononucleosis. Playing in 2002 on a medical exemption, Tryon missed 17 of 22 cuts, failed to keep his card and has struggled almost everywhere he has played since.

"I feel like I have a lot of talent," he said at one point during his odyssey. "I can really play well for one day, but I have a hard time finishing. I'll play good for a couple of rounds, or I'll be eight-under through 12 or 13 holes, then I'll play four-over through my last four; dumb stuff like that."

Victor Ciesielski plays three of the best rounds of his life, and still finishes at the bottom of the pile at a PGA Tour event. Ty Tryon becomes the youngest golfer to ever earn his Tour card, but ends up wandering in the golf wilderness. What's the message? That golf is hard? That professional golf is an almost impossible goal, even for the most talented?

Yes. But also to make sure you dream with your eyes wide open. So what does it take to play golf at the highest levels? In truth, a little bit of everything that you need to win a local junior tournament, only a little more of it. It's a vague answer, to be sure, but it's the truth. As you climb higher up the ladder, you will need to be a better driver, both in terms of power and accuracy; a more precise iron player; a more reliable scorer and a more creative short-game player. You will need the ability to hole the putts that are makeable, and make some of the ones that aren't so makeable too. Your game has to grow. And that's just to play college golf.

"To come to a Kent State, they better have a regional, national or even an international resume," says Herb Page, who's in his third decade coaching Division I golf at Kent State, and has had three players make it to the PGA Tour including British Open champion Ben Curtis. "You've got to be a proven competitor, and not just on the local level. It's kind of sad sometimes. You get all these resumes and the kids have won this and won that, but they don't have anything beyond local or regional experience.

"When they come to us, we want to polish them. At the NCAA DI level, we don't want to backtrack and fix their grip. We want them to come to us with strong fundamentals."

Want some facts? Try these on for size. Let's just consider playing golf at the National Collegiate Athletic Association level. United States college golf, in other words.

- There are generally eight to 12 players on a collegiate golf team.
- Five players qualify to play in each event. Obviously, if you do the math, a lot of pretty good golfers don't get to play or are stuck "on the bench."
- NCAA Division I men's golf programs have a maximum of 4.5 scholarships to award to players. Women's Division I programs have a maximum of six—a benefit of gender equity legislation that requires schools to offer as many overall athletic scholarships to women as they do for men.
- Coaches for NCAA teams get hundreds of application requests for golf scholarships. Those they choose to provide scholarships to have proven themselves in junior and amateur competition, winning events at the regional, state, national and even international levels.
- Being a student-athlete requires top-notch time-management skills. Daily practices are the norm, and travel during the fall and spring competitive seasons

means missing classes on a regular basis. It's up to the students to maintain their academic standing despite these additional time demands.

But what about on the golf course? What does it take to compete in college golf? According to Peter Sanders, creator of ShotByShot.com, a Stamford, Connecticut-based company that has analyzed more than 80,000 rounds of golf to determine the tendencies and habits of golfers at all levels, these are some of the standards your game has to meet if you expect to play at the college level:

- On a 35-yard wide fairway, college golfers will hit the short grass about nine times in a typical round, or 64%.
- They can fly the ball about 250 yards and produce an average ball speed of 160 miles an hour and a clubhead speed of 105 miles per hour with a driver.
- They only hit the ball into severe trouble or out of play (OB, penalty or advancement situation) about once every 20 drives, or less than once per round.
- NCAA players hit about 12.2 greens in regulation per round.
- They make about three birdies per round, and their average birdie putt is 18 feet.
- Their iron play is consistent. They find severe trouble (OB, water, unplayable) about once in every 10 rounds.
- Their short-game skills are very strong. Greenside sand shots are played to within eight feet 48% of the time.

- Three-putts are rare, about once every 35 holes played or on 3% of their total holes played.
- They make 90% of their putts under three feet, and make 56% of their 'scoring putts' between four and 10 feet.
- They get up-and-down 59% of the time within 50 yards, excluding sand shots and shots with a putter.

In general, playing golf at the NCAA Division I level is serious business. Golfers who play on scholarship have a competitive average of 71.9 and play courses that measure 6,800 yards. They are legitimately 0 or 'scratch' handicaps or better. NCAA Division I Men's Individual Champions are +4 handicaps!

Even more daunting is the gap that exists between players at that level and the PGA Tour, where most college golfers would like to play, at least in their mind's eye. There are more than 300 Men's Division I programs and about 3,400 players. Much less than 1% of all collegiate golfers will have successful careers as touring professionals. In the decade since Tiger Woods won the 1996 NCAA individual championship, only two NCAA champions—Charles Howell III and Ryan Moore—made the jump from college to the PGA Tour in one season. At any given time, there are over 1,000 full-time, professional golfers on the PGA, European, Nationwide, Asian, Australian, South African, South American and Canadian Tours. Most of them would do anything to get the 50 or so new spots that open up on the PGA Tour in any given season. Which is why you should keep in mind that there is more in life than golf.

"I've coached 29 years and we've had some exceptional players. I have five guys in the top 600 or 700 in the world, and no one knows who they are," says Page, member of the Golf Coaches of America Hall of Fame and Kent State coach. "My point is, golf is the hardest sport in the world to make it to the top level. Guys playing on the Nationwide Tour and the European PGA Tour are premier, elite players. I've got a guy, Peter Laws, playing on the Gateway Tour. No one has ever heard of him and he's one of the top 700 players in the world.

"That's why it's important to remember it's more than just becoming a better golfer and chasing that dream. It's about a good education, it's about friendships and social skills and team work. They can take those lessons anywhere they go in life."

USGA HANDICAPS

BY TIGER WOODS' STANDARDS, 2003 WASN'T A PARTICULARLY GOOD YEAR. HE WON FIVE TOURNAMENTS, BUT NO MAJORS. BUT BY ANYONE ELSE'S STANDARDS, IT WAS PRETTY IMPRESSIVE. SO TOO WAS HIS HANDICAP, AS CALCULATED BY GOLF DIGEST BASED ON THE YARDAGE OF THE TOURNAMENT LAYOUTS HE PLAYED THAT SEASON. HE'D HAVE TO GIVE A SCRATCH GOLFER AN AVERAGE OF EIGHT SHOTS FOR 18 HOLES.

COMPETITIVE HANDICAPS, AS CALCULATED BY GOLF DIGEST:

TIGER WOODS	+8.5
JIM FURYK	+7.2
PHIL MICKELSON	+6.0
MIKE WEIR	+6.0
FRED COUPLES	+5.6
TOM PERNICE (TOP 30)	+5.3
J.P. HAYES (TOP 125)	+4.3
LORENA OCHOA	+3.0
MATT HILL (NCAA CHAMPION)	+4.5

Don't believe him? Consider this case. In the late 1950s a tall, burly, talented golfer enrolled at the University of Indiana. He was, by all accounts, a solid college golfer, occasionally an exceptional one. He was playing on a good team in a good conference. There was one problem. Big-10 conference rival Ohio State University had this heavy-set blonde kid who simply would not be beaten. His contemporary at the University of Indiana played the kid from Ohio State 22 times, and lost every time. Understandably, the kid from Indiana decided that if he couldn't even beat this kid from Ohio State, how could he expect to compete on the PGA Tour? Instead of a career in golf, he focused on his studies and graduated with a degree in physics, eventually going to work for NASA helping put people into outer space. Ultimately, he was able to bring together his life-long passion for golf with his knack for scientific inquiry. Merging his two strengths helped Dave Pelz become one of the leading instructors in golf today, and a wealthy man.

The kid he couldn't beat at Ohio State? That was Jack Nicklaus. The point is: There are many routes to excellence. Golf can be your path to excellence, or a conduit that leads you places you never thought possible.

There are approximately 600,000 people working in the golf industry in the United States alone. There are 28,000 PGA Club Professionals and countless more involved in the game, ranging from equipment designers to sales people to course superintendents. Very few of them ever played golf professionally, but all have made a life in golf.

So, whatever the journey, its worthwhile having the facts on your side. Facts are facts, as they say. And no matter how worthy your game, the facts are worthy of your consideration. Because even if you choose the rare air of U.S. college golf—or the professional ranks—there is no guarantee that golf will choose you.

3

WHAT IS A GOLF COACH
AND WHERE CAN I GET ONE?

IN GOLF TODAY, coaches are sometimes as well known as the players themselves. Some are even known by a single name alone, giving them the kind of notoriety in golf circles that Brazilian soccer stars (Pele); boxers (Ali); entertainers (Madonna) and yes, even some golfers (Tiger) have come to enjoy in the pop culture pantheon.

When a golfer says he's been working with Butch, we know he means Butch Harmon, Tiger's former coach. When someone speaks about getting together with Led, it's David Leadbetter, who counts Michelle Wie as only his latest famous client. Those who follow the women's game closely know Pia is Pia Nilson, the den mother of Swedish golf and the friend, coach and confidante of Annika (another one-namer), the greatest female player of her generation, and possibly ever. Phil Mickelson couldn't get over that major championship hurdle until he hooked up with short-game guru (and former rocket scientist) Dave (Pelz), despite the best efforts of long-game expert Rick (Smith).

But golf instruction was around long before The Golf Channel's *Academy Live* helped turn teachers into stars. There are those who think the greatest—or at least the wisest—

golf instructor of all time was a gentle wee man from Texas named Harvey Penick. Penick had such a knack for making the complicated seem plain that he was able to distill his wisdom into a famous instruction manual that is short on drills and diagrams, but long on gems of insight that can mean more in a few words than a thousand words worth of pictures. He touched some great golfers in his time, but always lightly: "Suppose you are strolling along the road with a walking stick in your hand. You see an old tin can in the road," he explained in a typical anecdote. "You decide on impulse to give the can a hearty two-handed whack that will knock it into the grass. How do you do it? Do you tense up and worry about keeping your head still? Of course you don't, but your fundamentals are always sound when you whack a tin can. That's the freewheeling feeling you should have when you hit a golf ball." Sometimes it's important to keep it simple.

Ben Hogan was Tiger Woods until Tiger Woods came along—a model of golf efficiency who won everything in sight when he was at his peak in the mid-1950s. He was a famously self-made golfer, preferring to find his game in the dirt of the practice range, as he liked to say. People who were serious about learning about golf came to him, not the other way around. His book *Five Lessons: The Modern Fundamentals of Golf* is a classic piece of golf instruction that was ahead of its time when it was published in 1957. It was so influential that not one but two famous current teachers have revisited his teachings in recent years: David Leadbetter published *The Fundamentals of Hogan*, co-written with Lorne Rubenstein; while Jim McLean issued a video, *Ben Hogan: The Golf Swing*.

Some golfers change instructors every time they miss a few cuts, it seems. Jack Nicklaus worked with Jack Grout, the head professional at Scioto Counry Club, from the time he started golf at age 10 until Grout's death in 1989. All Nicklaus did was win 18 major titles and set a standard so high it's no wonder players since have put more and more faith in instructors to help them reach it. That said, it's worth noting Nicklaus's take on the matter: "I never called him once from a tournament," Nicklaus says. "I didn't need to call him every five minutes. I had to learn how to correct myself, which is the antithesis of the way it is today. For me it was more like the way it was with Bobby Jones. Jones told me that he became a good player when he didn't have to run back to [his teacher] Stewart Maiden."

Tiger Woods stopped working with Butch Harmon just when it seemed his game was as close to perfection as any golfer before or since. After winning seven of 11 majors he played between 1999 and 2002, Woods went into what, for him at least, was a slump, going winless in his next 10 major championship starts. In the meantime, he was working with Hank Haney, a well-respected instructor who was hardly a household name. Woods stuck with him and, in 2006, enjoyed as fruitful a stretch as he even he has ever known. He won six consecutive PGA Tour starts, including the British Open and the PGA Championship, while playing 24 rounds of golf in 113-under par, or an average of 4.7 strokes under par over 24 rounds of championship golf. Woods and Haney, questioned and doubted for their willingness to tinker with greatness, resisted every urge to say "I told you so" to all the people who wondered at their wisdom, or lack of it. But revenge is sweet. These days in professional golf, when someone refers to a coach as 'Hank,' everyone knows they mean Hank Haney.

But what do those coaches do? What should your coach do? How do you find one? How do you know he's the right one? How much do you pay him or her? How often do you see them?

Before answering these and other important questions, it's worth taking a moment to define a coach's role as it relates to serious junior golf, or any serious sporting activity. Obviously an important focus in golf or any other sport is technique. If the goal is to play your best golf in a competitive arena, you need a swing (and putting stroke and short game) that can be repeated under pressure. There is no getting around it. Looking good on the range or goofing around with friends is one thing. Maintaining your fundamentals when you need to par the final hole in a tournament is another. And in golf it's easy to get overwhelmed with technical talk as golfers and coaches alike try to use words and concepts to solve golf's basic problem: how to hit the ball solidly and control your distance, direction, trajectory and spin when you absolutely must. And then do it again.

A good golf coach should bring much more to the relationship than notions about swing plane and grip because there's more to hitting the ball solidly when you absolutely must than just swing plane and grip. It's about completing a journey that turns potential into accomplishment and hope into true confidence. Technique is only part of the trip.

Consider the root of the word *coach*. In the days before sweet rides, big rims and bumpin' sound sytems, a coach was a vehicle, a horse-drawn carriage that moved people from their starting point to their desired destination. A good golf coach uses all means at his disposal to take his charge to where they want to go. Does that mean if your goal is to play on the LPGA Tour or the PGA Tour, a good coach will get you there? No. It means that a good coach will help you achieve your potential, wherever that potential takes you. But a good coach does more than identify glitches in your swing. Golf coaches are agents of change with a focus on inspiring athletes to learn, train, develop, measure, evaluate and grow as golfers and people. The best coaches help their students learn how to coach themselves through challenges in golf and in life. And, ultimately, how to use that knowledge to coach others.

Coaches are responsible for:

- Helping the athlete better understand who he is as an individual
- Identifying the goals of the athlete
- Objectively measuring the skill levels of the player
- Providing advice and strategies for improving the swing technique and fundamentals
- Facilitating the establishment of a detailed success strategy that leads to the achievement of the desired outcomes
- Educating and supporting parents
- Communicating openly with athletes, parents, golf officials and collegiate coaches
- Encouraging and nurturing the athlete both on and off the course
- Providing specific feedback

So, like the game itself, coaching excellence is far more complex than most people know. A good coach doesn't merely arrive on the practice range, roll some balls onto the turf and say, "Go to it." And a good coach doesn't tell his client what, when and how. Instead they enter into an on-going dialogue with the golfer, working together to establish a strategy for success according to objectives that the athlete has set for himself. In this way, the route the golfer will follow towards their potential belongs to the athlete—they own it, are responsible for it and accountable to it. The coach is there to make sure it's the right route, and to act as a guide along the way.

And there is a distinction between an average teaching professional and a coach who has the experience and knowledge required to meet the demands and expectations of competitive golfers. Helping a beginning golfer break 100 or a bogey golfer become comfortable in a corporate tournament is a vital part of helping people enjoy golf and get more from the game. But responding to talented junior players and helping them develop a foundation that turns them into scratch players or beyond requires a specialist's eye for detail and insight about the finer points of the game and its pressures. Teachers with these types of qualities are in demand and charge between $100 and $150 an hour or a season-long or year-long comprehensive program for a flat fee. It's not cheap, but consider the cost of hiring an amateur.

An indication that a coach is not right for you is if there is a promise for a quick fix for what ails you or a suggestion that there will be a fundamental change in your game on the strength of a quick session on the range. Learning golf is not a one-time event. Developing your game requires an on-going investment of commitment, discipline and knowledge.

Helping players learn the game should come in three main stages:

1. **The first is the assessment stage.** It's tempting for players to believe that they are one good swing thought away from playing their best golf, and it's sometimes tempting for coaches to put a Band-aid on a blister rather than point out that the reason you have sore

feet is because of a problem with your gait. But with an eye on long-term goals, a good instructor will assess the range of factors that are contributing unwanted strokes to a player's score. If you go to a doctor's office complaining of a fever and sore throat, wouldn't you be disappointed if the doctor made the obvious diagnosis without first making sure they weren't symptoms of a deeper and more serious illness? Similarly, in the assessment stage, a coach should consider all aspects of a golfer's game, rather than simply 'diagnosing' that grip that he's convinced is causing your deathly hook. By fully assessing your game, including equipment analysis, on-course observation, skills testing; bio-mechanical analysis; video analysis; physical screen and mental skills inventories, a top instructor can accurately identify your current level and begin to formulate a plan that will elevate your game to the next level and beyond. Quality teaching must be preceded by quality assessment.

2. **The next stage is the process of providing players with solutions to the cause-and-effect relationships that are limiting their performance.** This is where teaching begins. Using everything from videotape instruction to written materials, top teachers use a range of strategies to give players the concepts they need to improve their game and the drills and practice techniques to learn them. Different students process the same basic information in different ways. A good teacher can use varying metaphors, pictures, stories, exercises and analogies to find a way to connect with different

players and provide them with the knowledge of what they need to do to improve.

3. **Once the assessments have been made and the lessons implemented, teaching gives way to coaching.** In this context, coaching involves helping the player take what they have been taught in 'the classroom' (on the lesson tee or during practice rounds) and successfully transfer that learning to the golf course in a competitive environment. It's this transition—from skill acquisition to being able to use your skills and techniques under pressure—that separates the competitive golfer from those who simply play golf. Not everyone can make the transition or is willing to put in the required effort to become a golfer with a pretty swing to one that is also a tough competitor. At this stage, a golfer serious about making the leap will likely need to make sure they're working with a golf coach and not an instructor. The difference? Think of a golf instructor as your Phys Ed teacher: He's perfectly capable of introducing the rules and fundamentals of basketball, but he's not necessarily the right person to coach the school team to a championship.

Similarly, a swing teacher is what you need when you are introduced to the game, someone who can make sure you understand the fundamentals of hitting a golf ball at a target. But as you progress through the junior ranks, you will need to make sure you're aligned with a golf teacher that specializes in high performance coaching and its fundamental goal: getting the ball into the hole the fastest against a field of top players trying to do the same thing. If you can't transfer those skills you're developing on the range to the golf course, all that work on the range doesn't do much good.

In that context, coaching expands to include supervising students during practice and providing feedback that will accelerate the learning process; creating or identifying training drills that will help the golfer on the golf course, not just the lesson tee; and providing on-course coaching to help improve decision making and executing the required shots in specific situations. Simply assessing a problem and teaching a solution do not lead to lower scores. Coaching the golfer to take those new skills to the golf course, and ultimately have the improvement show up on the scorecard, completes the cycle.

And because this is golf, once one cycle of assessment, teaching and coaching is completed, it simply means that it is time to start another cycle. A good coach helps with all that. And who knows? Stick with a good coach through enough of these cycles and you might become so good you'll only need one name.

FIVE THINGS TO ASK A PROSPECTIVE COACH

1. **What are your credentials?** Not all teaching professionals are created equal, which isn't to say one is better than the other, but some coaches have taken steps to prepare themselves for the demands of teaching elite players. Ideally your coach should be a Class A PGA Professional, for starters. In addition, your coach should be able to demonstrate a commitment to refining his or her craft to better meet your needs. The PGA offers a range of teaching specialization courses, some of which

emphasize high performance. Which courses has your instructor taken? Similarly, does he or she routinely attend professional workshops put on by recognized leaders in the field? Because high performance coaching involves more than simply the golf swing, does your instructor have a background in sports science or physical education? Are they comfortable providing information about nutrition and fitness as it pertains to golf, or do they have working relationships with experts in the field?

2. **What type of experience do you have?** Before you commit to what ideally will be a long-term relationship with your coach, be comfortable that they have taken others to the places you want your golf game to go. Does the coach have a proven record of success working with top juniors? Has the coach developed players who have won important events locally, regionally or nationally? Is the coach able to take good players— low single-digit handicappers, for example—and turn them into scratch players or better? Have his or her players progressed through the ranks of junior golf and earned scholarships at respected golf programs? Can I speak with some players who have worked with you in the past?

3. **Do you have the time available to work with me?** Top coaches are usually in demand, with more players seeking their services than they have time to help. Some coaches offer an opportunity to enroll in a season-long program that allows for meetings on a weekly basis. A good program should run about nine months of the year

and carry the golfer from pre-season preparation right through the peak of the competitive year and cover all aspects of the game as it relates to competitive golf—everything from fitness and nutrition to rules of golf. If the coach doesn't offer a season-round program, can he or she commit to meeting with you on a weekly basis that's convenient for both of you? Is the coach willing to come and observe you in competitive situations? Does he or she make time for on-course lessons? And keep in mind, in life you generally get what you pay for, and golf is no exception. Coaches who work with top competitive players typically charge $100 an hour or more. It's reasonable to budget $3,500 to $5,000 a season for coaching.

4. **What type of teaching facility and teaching aids can you provide?** If you're going to work on your game year-round, or close to it, you need facilities that provide for it. Does your coach have access to practice venues that are weather protected? You will need to be working hard on your putting and short game skills, so make sure your coach can provide an opportunity for you to chip, putt and work on your sand game on a regular basis. Increasingly, technology is becoming part of every good coach's arsenal. The coach should have ready access to, and be comfortable using, video teaching aids and advanced club-fitting techniques

5. **Will we be able to work well together?** Like many things in golf, you can plan and prepare all you want, but at some point you have to go with how you feel. Choosing a golf coach isn't that much different. When all the research is

done, it's important that you feel comfortable with your coach and he feels comfortable with you. The two of you will be spending a lot of time together in the next few years and it should be enjoyable. There is room for smiles and laughs in golf, even when going about the business of improving.

A good coach should be able to expand your understanding, not only of your golf swing, but of your character and personality, helping you identify qualities that help you excel and others that are holding you back. Some coaches teach only one method and expect you to adapt to their tried and true ways. Others are comfortable to adapt to the way you feel most comfortable learning. Neither approach is 'right' but one may be more 'right' for you. In the end, the right coach can help you become a better golfer and much more, so choose wisely.

A COACH'S TALE

Herb Page has coached golf at Kent State during four different decades. He's had players win on the PGA Tour, win majors, and win at life away from the golf course. Here's what a coach looks for in a player:

"To come to Kent State, they better have a state, national or even international resume. You've got to be a proven competitor, and not just on the local level. It's kind of sad sometimes, you get all these resumes and the kids have won this and won that, but they don't have anything beyond local or regional experience.

"When they come to us, we want to polish them. At the NCAA DI level, we don't want to backtrack and fix their grip. We want them to come to us with strong fundamentals. But it's about more than golf, they need to have a strong academic record. If you play for us or Florida or UCLA, you're only allowed to play so many days. Even if you go all the way to the national championships, that's 12 major tournaments in a year. During the rest of the year you become a person. You go to college and have an academic, athletic and social life. You want a balance.

"It's an individual sport, but it's a team game. I have guys like British Open champion and former Kent State golfer Ben Curtis call me and say the best four years of their lives were in college, traveling with their buddies and having fun. But they only realize it when they're done and out on Tour, ordering room service. So you're looking for people who understand the chemistry of the team.

"I've coached 29 years and we've had some exceptional players. I have five guys in the top 600 or 700 in the world, and no one knows who they are. My point is, golf is the hardest sport in the world to make it to the top level. Guys playing on the Nationwide Tour and the European PGA Tour are premier, elite players. I've got a guy, Peter Laws, playing on the Gateway Tour. No one has ever heard of him and he's one of the top 700 players in the world.

"That's why it's important to remember it's more than just becoming a better golfer and chasing that dream. It's about a good education; it's about friendships and social skills and team work. They can take those lessons anywhere they go in life."

4

Carpenters are Only as Good as Their Tools

It's a common mistake and easy to make. Every Sunday afternoon during golf season someone will knock in a 10-foot birdie putt to win a tournament. Or hit a wedge stiff to set up an easy par with their playing partner breathing down their neck. Or thread the fairway with a softly fading drive that catches the landing area just so, giving someone a chance to attack the green on their second shot and set up a winning eagle. And then there's applause and congratulatory kisses or maybe a jump in the lake. And, of course, a trophy, a word from our sponsors and a big cardboard cheque with lots of zeroes.

Clearly professional golf tournaments are won on Sunday. Usually on the back nine. Often on the last hole. Everyone with a remote and cable knows that. Happens every week.

Except it's not true. Professional golf tournaments are just as likely to be won on Tuesdays, in the back of a customized tractor trailer, far away from the fairways and the crowds and the cameras. It's on Tuesdays that the PGA Tour and LPGA Tour's version of a Formula One pit crew roll into town. Bearing the logos of all the major manufacturers, they are the home to the club technicians that service those that wield their company's drivers, irons and putters like high-tech magic wands. Get it right—and that means just right—and their staff player can tee it up on Thursday with the most important piece of equipment in any golfer's arsenal: confidence.

Professional players will go to nearly any length to make sure that the equipment they're using gives them the best chance to play their best golf. The examples are endless. In 2006 Phil Mickelson was trying to win his second Masters and third major title. Part of the genius of Augusta is the way the course flows left and right like a gently meandering river. There have been players with predominantly right-to-left ball flights that have won there. There have been players who play the ball left-to-right that have won there too. But the golfers that have had the most success at The Masters have been those that can shape the ball in both directions off the tee and best set themselves up for the all-important second shots into the greens, where it's often better to be putting from 20 feet on the correct side of the hole than to be 10 feet away but on the wrong side. It's a power course, but it demands precision.

By this time, Mickelson had a well-earned reputation as a bit of an equipment geek. He even got himself in a little bit of trouble in 2004 when he dared point out that Tiger Woods, of all people, was playing with inferior equipment because of his refusal to embrace the latest driver technology. "He hates that I can fly it past him now," Mickelson said in an interview with *GOLF Magazine*. "He has a faster swing speed than I do, but he has inferior equipment. Tiger is the only player who is good enough to overcome the equipment he's stuck with." He may have stepped on Woods' toes a little bit, but he was right. Woods' amazing run of success during the 2005 and 2006 seasons—he finished third or higher in 22 of his 36 starts, including 14 wins and four majors—

coincided with him switching to the latest generation big-headed driver and regaining the distance advantage that had ebbed away ever so slightly.

Heading into the 2006 Masters, Mickelson had a revelation: Rather than trying to use one driver to hit fades *and* draws, why not use two drivers? One was set up to favor draws and another to set up fades, which is a more controlled tee-shot. He put the two drivers in his bag at the Bell South and won by 13 shots; kept them in at the Masters a week later and won his second green jacket and third major.

The temptation might be for everyone else to follow Mickelson's lead, except that it's easier said than done. Even if you had the nearly $1,000 you would need to buy two versions of the Callaway Fusion FT-3, a regular Joe or Joanne off the street would need another $400 to buy the Mitsubishi Diamana shafts he used. Most significantly you would need the time and expertise of those folks in the Callaway truck who fine-tuned Mickelson's drivers so he could switch between them without having to adjust his swing. For example, because Mickelson's draw driver had a 46-inch shaft as opposed to the 45-inch shaft in his fader, the clubhead on the longer club was about 6 grams lighter and the longer shaft was slightly stiffer than the shorter one. Mickelson deserves full credit for his 2006 Masters win for playing some of the most solid golf of his career down the stretch on Sunday. But he wouldn't have been able to do it without some good work in the truck on Tuesday.

The point of all this, of course, is that in this day and age, any serious golfer needs to emulate, as closely as possible, not only the practice habits of the world's best players, but also the commitment they make to having the best equipment and the equipment that suits their games the best too. But—and this is a big but—just because Mickelson uses a particular brand of club and Tiger Woods another doesn't mean those are the clubs you should use. In fact, it's important to remember that the clubs on the commercials and in the pro shops aren't the clubs they're using either. The basics might be the same, but each club has been tweaked and adjusted and tested to make sure they meet the specifications of that player alone. It's not enough these days to walk into a pro-shop with a credit card and buy the most expensive set of clubs available. Hopefully, they will be high quality, but they may not be the best clubs for you.

The goals for your equipment choices should be threefold:

1. **First, they must be of a good enough quality that the clubs themselves provide consistent performance.** The best clubs provide accurate feedback on why a shot went wrong or right. Inferior equipment alone can sometimes be the cause of a less-than-ideal shot because it doesn't give the player the feel required to make precise shots under pressure—the same input doesn't yield the same result on a consistent basis—or because the physical limits of the club aren't up to the stress put on them by a high performance player.

2. **Second, the equipment must fit the player perfectly.** Not close to perfectly, not 'good enough,' but perfectly. It only makes sense, when you think about it. Why spend time and effort honing your swing mechanics, improving your fitness and developing the mental discipline required to play consistent golf in competitive conditions only to have equipment

that requires you to swing a little differently from one club to the next? Or worse, fit you in such a way that you're grooving a less-than-ideal swing to match ill-fitting clubs?

3. **Third, you should love your equipment.** Their look, feel and sound should please you. They are a part of you when you play golf. You spend hours working with them. You rely on them when the pressure is on. Aesthetics aren't everything, but your clubs should make you pleased every time you look in your bag.

CUSTOM FITTING—A RECIPE FOR SUCCESS

The best way to the make sure you're getting the equipment that is best for you is to have the entire set custom fitted. No two golfers are the same and no two swings alike, so if you try to buy equipment that is 'off-the-rack' it's inevitable that the fit won't be as precise as clubs that are tuned to your individual specifications. Along those lines, you should be measured for your clubs in conditions that are as close to 'real life' as possible.

The first thing anyone does when they buy shoes is get up and walk around in them, right? Similarly, you want to get your clubs fitted so that they fit you when you're swinging and making contact with a golf ball, not just when standing at address. This process is called *dynamic fitting*, where you go to a practice range and hit shots while a trained professional watches, gaining feedback from your comments, the flight of the ball and the shape of the divots you are leaving. If someone wants to fit you for clubs without seeing you hit, or seeing you hit into a net or indoors by relying on calibrated machines, they're not getting the full picture of your swing and the way it interacts with the club.

Getting custom fit clubs is an exciting process. It's a matter of removing one of the countless variables that must be accounted for to make good golf shots. Some you can't control—the way the ball sits in the rough; the wind conditions; the presence of hazards or the placement of the flag. Having equipment that works for you is a variable you can control. The cost is relatively insignificant—typically the same price as an hour-long lesson. Often a teaching professional will waive the fee if you buy clubs from him. It takes about 30 minutes to an hour to be fitted for irons and an additional hour to be fitted for a driver, fairway metals and wedges. The clubs themselves don't cost any more than those you would buy 'off-the-rack'—you're only paying for the fitting session—and most manufacturers will provide your custom clubs in a week or less upon getting the order. Arrive at your fitting session ready to practice, wearing your golf shoes, comfortable clothes and a glove. Come with an open mind as well.

THE ELEMENTS OF A GOOD FIT

There are four primary elements that go into making sure clubs are properly fitted:

1. **Club Length.** The first step in a fitting session in most cases is determining how long the clubs should be. There is no fixed answer. Simply put, your clubs should be a length that allows you to assume the best athletic possible position at address and remain there throughout the entire swing, particularly at impact.

The length of your clubs should never require you to adjust your swing technique or compromise your balance. With the help of a club fitting system (provided by the equipment manufacturers), the professional conducting your fitting session will have you hit balls with 6-irons of various lengths (6-irons are roughly the mid-point between your driver and wedges, and have enough loft and impart enough sidespin to provide reliable feedback). The clubfaces have tape on them so the professional can see where the ball was at impact and adjustments are made—some as small as a quarter-inch—until you find the length that allows contact in the center of the clubface most consistently.

2. **Lie Angle.** The lie angle is the distance (measured in degrees) between the heel of the club and the ground. Properly fitted irons strike the turf squarely after contact, leaving a nice, square divot. If the toe or heel of the club hit the ground first, the shot will be hit off line. Just two degrees difference in the lie angle can result in a miss of more than 20 feet with a 5-iron. This is a particular case where it's important to be hitting balls outside while being fitted. How the clubhead lies on the turf at address doesn't tell the whole story, or even part of it. The club's shaft bows dramatically just prior to impact. The key is to make sure that the lie angle is correct for that moment, not when the club is at rest during address. Finding the right lie angle starts with tape being added to the bottom of a club of the correct length. You then hit shots off a 'lie board'—a glass plastic sheet that is place on the ground in the

PUTTERS NEED FITTING TOO

CUSTOM FITTING DOESN'T START WITH YOUR WEDGES AND END WITH YOUR DRIVER. AT LEAST IT SHOULDN'T. THERE IS NO QUESTION THAT DISCOVERING YOUR OPTIMAL CLUB "SPECS" FACILITATES ENHANCED PERFORMANCE AND ENJOYMENT FOR GOLFERS. MOST GOLFERS WILL NOT CONSIDER INVESTING IN NEW CLUBS UNLESS THEY ARE CUSTOM FIT. SO WHY DO SO MANY GOLFERS PLAY WITH PUTTERS WHICH ARE TOO LONG FOR THEM?

PUTTING ACCOUNTS FOR ABOUT 40% OF ALL STROKES FOR ALL LEVELS OF GOLFERS. HOWEVER, PUTTER FITTING HAS LAGGED BEHIND IRON AND DRIVER/FAIRWAY METAL FITTING. A PUTTER THAT ISN'T PROPERLY FIT FORCES YOU TO COMPROMISE FUNDAMENTALS AND TECHNIQUE. THAT MEANS MORE MISSED PUTTS.

GOLF MAGAZINE TOP 100 TEACHER TODD SONES, A RENOWNED PUTTING COACH AND RESEARCHER, SHARED SOME EXCELLENT RESEARCH AND INFORMATION USING THE PYTHAGOREAN THEOREM $(A^2 + B^2 = C^2)$ IN ORDER TO HELP GOLFERS ACCURATELY DETERMINE THE OPTIMAL LENGTH OF THEIR PUTTERS AND SUBSEQUENTLY AID THEM IN IMPROVING THEIR PUTTING TECHNIQUE AND PERFORMANCE IN FOUR EASY STEPS.

FIND THE OPTIMAL LENGTH OF YOUR PUTTER USING PYTHAGOREAN THEOREM $A^2 + B^2 = C^2$

STEP #1: SET UP IN THE PROPER POSTURE AS ILLUSTRATED.

STEP #2: DETERMINING MEASUREMENT "A^2" - THE DISTANCE FROM THE TOP WRIST CREASE DOWN TO THE GROUND. THIS IS "A^2" - THE VERTICAL LEG OF A TRIANGLE.

STEP #3: PLACE A MIRROR ON THE GROUND ON THE TARGET LINE. SET UP WITH THE EYES OVER THE BALL—"SEE" YOUR EYES

IN THE MIRROR—THEN HAVE THE "B2" MEASUREMENT TAKEN AS ILLUSTRATED. THIS MEASUREMENT BECOMES THE HORIZONTAL LEG OF A TRIANGLE.

STEP #4: ONCE THE VERTICAL LEG ("A2") AND HORIZONTAL LEG ("B2") OF THE TRIANGLE HAVE BEEN DETERMINED, THEN SQUARE THEM AND ADD THEM TOGETHER USING THE PYTHAGOREAN THEORY ($A^2 + B^2 = C^2$) TO CALCULATE THE DIAGONAL LEG OF THE TRIANGLE ("C2"). "C2" IS THE OPTIMAL PUTTER LENGTH FOR A GOLFER. FOR EXAMPLE, IF A GOLFER'S WRIST TO GROUND MEASUREMENT IS = 33" (A2), AND THEIR TOES TO GOLF

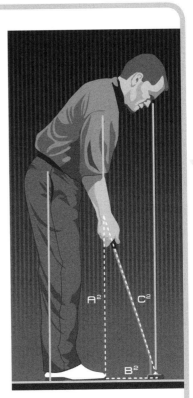

BALL MEASUREMENT IS = 10" (B2), THEN THE OPTIMAL LENGTH FOR THEIR PUTTER IS (A2—33 x 33) 1089 + (B2—10x10) 100 = 34.48 INCHES (C2—1189). THIS GOLFER IS LIKELY TO PERFORM BEST WITH A PUTTER THAT IS 34.5" IN LENGTH.

WHEN A PUTTER IS THE PROPER LENGTH, IT SHOULD SIMPLY CONNECT THE DISTANCE FROM WHERE THE EYES HIT THE GROUND AND WHERE THE ARMS HANG NATURALLY UNDER THE SHOULDERS. THIS ENABLES THE GOLFER TO DEVELOP SOUND PUTTING MECHANICS AND GET THEIR EYES IN AN IDEAL POSITION FOR AIMING AND GAINING A TRUE PERSPECTIVE OVER THEIR PUTTS.

impact area, the ball on top. The marks left on the tape will indicate what adjustments are needed to find the ideal lie angle. The goal is to show marks in the centre of the club, indicating the ball is being hit square toward the target. If the club is too upright, the marks will be on the heel and the ball will fly to the right. If the club is too flat, the marks will be on the toe and the ball will fly left.

3. **Shaft Flex.** The shaft is perhaps the most important component of a club, some say that it provides the club its heartbeat because it allows the energy of your swing to be transferred to the clubhead and the ball. It acts like a spring in the sense that it bends and twists as it absorbs the power of your swing and then unloads all the accumulated power at impact. There is a wide range of choice for shafts and it is up to you and the professional helping you at your fitting session to determine the best one for your game.

   There is a common misconception that swing speed alone determines the shaft flex—regular, stiff or extra stiff, for example—you need. Swing speed is important, but just as important is how you arrive at your swing speed. Take the styles of Ernie Els and Nick Price. Both have swing speeds around 110 miles per hour. But Els, one of the bigger golfers on the PGA Tour, has a long, fluid motion that builds up power slowly and gradually. His return to the ball from the top of his back swing is smooth and steady, and as a result the stress on the shaft of his club is relatively low. Price's swing is famously quick, the transition almost violent.

The transition from back swing to down swing puts a huge load on the shaft. The result is that Els, a bigger and more powerful golfer, requires a shaft that is less stiff than the one used by Price.

Any discussion of the golf shaft naturally raises the question of shaft composition. Do I need graphite or steel? Or some combination? This, again, is something your coach or the profes-sional helping you fit your clubs can guide you through. But the basic differences include:

Steel Shafts

- Consistent flex from shaft to shaft
- Less expensive than graphite
- Significantly heavier at soft, medium and stiff flexes than graphite
- Performs better at various swing speeds—i.e., ball flight and distance control better on partial shots
- Creates a lower launch angle and ball flight than graphite
- Can come with shock dampening properties
- Preferred shaft for irons by most professionals and top amateurs

Graphite Shafts

- Extremely difficult for manufacturers to make a "matched set" of graphite shafts for irons.
- Lighter and have more "torque" at lower flexes. This allows recreational players to control the club easier, swing it faster than with steel, and to hit the ball with more spin and a higher trajectory.
- Top quality graphite shafts are expensive.
- Creates more spin and a higher ball flight. This

can be an advantage to some players (generally 'average golfers') and a disadvantage to others (players with high swing speeds).

- Works best at an all-out swing speed. Top players often use graphite on their 'all-out clubs,' drivers, fairway metals and hybrids.

- Finesse or specialty shots, typically hit with irons, don't always come off as well or as predictably with graphite. Ball flight has a tendency to balloon into the wind for strong players.

4. **Grip Size:** The thickness of a player's grips is an important element of proper fitting that is often overlooked. Making the grips bigger or smaller is simply a matter of installing grips of the required thickness or adding or deleting the amount of tape ('wraps') under the grip until the right thickness is achieved. There are a range of types or styles of grips. Some are more durable than others. Choose one based on its feel and look.

DON'T SPOIL THE RECIPE—
EQUIPMENT PITFALLS TO AVOID

- They look good, and the price looks too good to be believed. Buyer beware. If you are considering clubs that look like top brand equipment but cost a fraction of the price, think again. Chances are they're 'knock-offs'—hastily manufactured fakes that look like the real thing but aren't. The lofts, centers of gravity, swing weights, shaft quality and other components are likely inconsistent from club to club and unacceptable for a top golfer. If price is an issue, talk to your golf professional, he may be able to guide you to top quality used equipment.

- Once you've spent the time and money to get custom-fitted equipment, don't be tempted to alter them on your own. Cutting down or adding length to a club alters the balance (swing weight) of a club and also changes the shaft flex and the lie angle. Don't substitute a graphite shaft for a steel shaft, or vice versa. The clubheads in each case are weighted to be used with either graphite or steel, not both. Similarly, adding lead tape or drilling holes in clubheads to customize your feel will only distort the design properties and performance of the club. Millions have been invested in research and development for top grade equipment. It's highly unlikely you can improve on that on your own.

- Finally, no matter how compelling the infomercial or how promising the claim, don't pick up the phone unless it's to call your PGA Professional.

And by the way, don't forget that equipment is only part of the equation. In 2007 Mickelson once again had two perfectly prepared drivers in his bag as he set out to defend his Masters title. But he came up short, undone by a modest hitting, relative unknown named Zach Johnson who won his first major, winning by two shots over the likes of Tiger Woods and Retief Goosen. And while his clubs were custom fitted too, it was his putter that was his magic wand as he needed only 112 putts for 72 holes.

KEYS FOR CHOOSING YOUR BEST BALL

1. THE BALL IS THE MOST IMPORTANT CLUB IN THE BAG. IT IS THE ONLY 'CLUB' THAT YOU USE ON EVERY SINGLE SHOT.

2. ACCORDINGLY, THE PERSON WHO IS FITTING YOU FOR YOUR CLUBS SHOULD IDEALLY TEST YOU WITH YOUR PREFERRED TYPE OF BALL OR SOMETHING SIMILAR TO MAKE SURE THE CLUB'S PERFORMANCE MATCHES WELL WITH YOUR PREFERRED BALL'S CHARACTERISTICS. TESTING NEW CLUBS WITH RANGE BALLS DOESN'T CUT IT.

3. DON'T CHOOSE YOUR BALL TYPE BASED ON OVERALL DISTANCE CHARACTERISTICS. PREMIUM BALLS ALL HAVE SIMILAR DISTANCE QUALITIES WITHIN A RANGE OF A FEW YARDS.

4. THE MOST IMPORTANT QUESTION: WHICH BALL GIVES YOU THE TOUCH AND CONTROL THAT ALLOWS YOU TO FEEL GOOD ABOUT YOUR SCORING SHOTS? KNOCK-DOWN AND HALF SHOTS, FLOP SHOTS, AND CHIPPING AND PUTTING ARE THE AREAS OF THE GAME WHERE YOU REALLY NEED TO BE COMFORTABLE WITH YOUR GOLF BALL.

5. PRICE ISN'T THE ULTIMATE OBSTACLE. IF YOUR BEST CHOICE IS MORE THAN YOU CAN AFFORD, THEN A GOOD TEACHING PROFESSIONAL SHOULD BE ABLE TO STEER YOU TO A SIMILAR PERFORMING BALL AT A LOWER PRICE POINT. FOR EXAMPLE, A GOOD ALTERNATIVE TO THE TITLEIST PRO V1 IS THE TITLEIST NXT TOUR, WHICH HAS COMPARABLE CHARACTERISTICS BUT IS SIGNIFICANTLY LESS EXPENSIVE.

5

The Art of Perfect Practice

IF SOMEONE WERE TO DESIGN the ideal golfer they would include a number of traits held by nearly all the top players. First would be the ability to hit the ball long and straight. Many things go into playing good golf, but being able to bang the ball a long way down the fairway means you are playing offense instead of defense. Next would come putting. A long drive and a mid-iron to 10 feet only pays off if you can roll in the 10-foot birdie putt at least some of the time; and those four footers for par count just as much. The ideal golfer would play with great tempo and rhythm, allowing them to master all the crafty in-between shots inside 100 yards that scoring requires. Great tempo and rhythm set apart the merely good players from the great.

You'd want all these things—power, touch, and a sense of calm under pressure. But more than anything you'd want a healthy dose of myelin. If you've never heard of myelin, you shouldn't worry. It's not something you can buy at a pro shop or a drugstore or even read about in a golf magazine. But people who study the brain, and in particular how the brain works as we learn new skills, believe myelin is the magic that enables talent to develop. So what am I talking about? Myelin is a sheath of fatty tissue that coats nerve fibers in the brain. Think of it like rubber insulation surrounding a copper wire. Myelin preserves the strength of electrical impulses that travel along the copper wire, or nerve fiber.

What does this have to do with golf? Or with playing piano or chess or tennis or any other activity that requires a lot of time and patience to master? The general theme is that when we're trying to do something difficult, like serve a tennis ball or make a good golf swing, the impulses in the brain that control the action are many and varied. The key to making the swing we want is to have the signals "travel at the right speed [and] arrive at the right time," says Dr. Douglas Fields, one of the world's leading experts in developmental neurobiology. In other words, if you're trying to hit a soft 9-iron downwind and your brain sends the signal to hit a regular 9-iron, you've just earned yourself a bogey, maybe worse.

And the difference between your brain sending the signals correctly and something going slightly wrong takes place in the time it takes a fly to flap its wings. Now here's the best part: the interesting thing about myelin is that its insulating qualities improve—it actually gets thicker—the more often the nerves it surrounds are called into action. And the thicker it gets, the more precisely the brain's signals travel, arriving at their destination at the proper time and in the proper sequence. In other words, the more myelin you have in the right parts of the brain, the better your chances of your soft 9-iron one-hopping to five feet below the hole.

And the most important thing about myelin? The more you practice, the more you get.

Any serious golfer is familiar with practice. It is fair to say that no one has ever achieved any reasonable proficiency in the game without working at it. But there is practice, and there is proper practice. There is going to practice because it's time to go to practice, and there is going to practice so engaged in what you are doing that nearly every moment is used to further perfect the skills you are trying to master. The old line about practice making perfect is a mistake. Practice makes permanent. Perfect practice makes perfect. And myelin: "What do good athletes do when they train? They send precise impulses along wires that give the signal to the myelin on that wire," says Dr. George Bartzokis, a professor of neurology at UCLA. "They end up, with all the training, with a super-duper wire—lots of bandwidth, a high-speed T-1 line. That's what makes them different than the rest of us."

Anders Ericsson, a professor of psychology at Florida State University is one of the world's leading experts on skill acquisition. He has spent most of his academic career studying practice and expert performance across many different activities (sports, music, chess, medicine) to learn why some people learn how to do things better than others and what the best way is to teach them. And while truly talented people can seem magical when compared to ordinary folk—anyone who has seen professional golfers in person usually can't help but be amazed at how good they are compared to even respectable recreational players—Ericsson says even the very best golfers or musicians can trace their success to deliberate practice aimed at mastering a specific task or groups of tasks.

What is deliberate practice? Ericsson defines it this way: "Being engaged in activities specifically designed to improve performance with full concentration."

And this is the part that separates those who dream about being a world class competitor in golf or any other sport from those who plan on it: Ericsson's research shows that it takes about

10 years or more of intense practice and training in a particular area to reach a level where you will be able to compete on a national or international level.

And consider this, according to Dr. Ericsson's research:

- Experts engage in deliberate practice for about four or five hours per day. And don't think that you can roll out of bed tomorrow, practice for four hours and be on your way. It takes time—and practice— to develop the ability to sustain the concentration required for deliberate practice. It's not just time, it's quality time.

- Once you accept the challenge of increasing the intensity, volume and quality of your practice, you accept another challenge: finding the proper balance between strain and rest as you pursue the limits of your performance.

- Despite best intentions, most people never reach their potential athletically or in other areas because they don't ever understand the highly refined, intense and deliberate practice approach required for elite performers.

- And practice doesn't stop. Putting in 10 good years of work from age 12 to age 22 might make you a solid college golfer or even a national or international level performer, but it guarantees little after that. All that work doesn't mean you can coast into future success. With some work, you can maintain that level, but to continue to improve, you need to continue the dedication to the practice that got you to that level in the first place.

So the challenge has been laid out in plain terms: Great golf—or at least the best golf you are capable of playing, doesn't come by accident. It doesn't happen because you really like to golf and play as often as you can. Reaching your potential requires a plan. The good news is you can make your next practice better than your last almost instantly. Heading out the door this afternoon? Here are a dozen tips to maximize your next practice:

1. **Don't hit too many balls.** This might sound strange, but hitting more balls can hurt, rather than help. If you find yourself 'raking and hitting,' simply lining up the next shot as soon as you hit the last, it's probably time to leave. Work with a goal in mind—developing a nice rhythm with your wedges, for example—and leave on a high note. Don't keep hitting until you are tired, sore and frustrated.

2. **Practice the way that suits you.** Golf is an individual sport; there is no single way to learn new skills. If you are working on refining a new shot, emphasize technique. If you are maintaining an existing skill, emphasize a creative approach. Find the balance between drills and playing that works for you, not someone you know.

3. **Practice for the right reasons.** Practice is an enjoyable time used to learn or maintain skills. It is not something you do to punish yourself for poor play, relieve guilt, or to please someone else. For the best players, practice is a privilege and a pleasure they enjoy returning to time and time again.

4. **That which is measured, can be improved.** Are you getting better? Maybe your scores don't say so yet, but by

keeping a journal to track your performance in practice you can see your progress, gain confidence and take that confidence to the course. Lower scores will follow.

5. **Resist over practicing.** Are you getting injuries or strains? Does going to practice feel like a duty? If it does, you're focused on results, "I want to shoot a good score," rather than process, "I'm going to focus on hitting good shots," and you might be practicing too much. Don't be afraid to take a break.

6. **Resist under practicing.** Are you playing poorly? Are you having trouble with your touch, timing and tempo? Do you tee it up feeling like you don't really deserve to perform your best? You might not be practicing enough.

7. **Practice like you play.** Use your imagination to put yourself in tough, competitive situations (leading your arch rival by a shot with a hole to play at your favorite tournament) and then practice your mental routine to help you hit confident shots or putts under pressure.

8. **Play like you practice.** Remember the way you felt while having an exceptionally good recreational round—were you relaxed, chatty, focused, yet loose? Whatever the case, challenge yourself to behave in competition the same way you do when you are practicing well.

9. **Don't be boring!** Golf requires a lot of thought and deliberation, but you are an athlete too. Spend some time in practice doing athletic things. Don't be afraid to tap into your 'right' brain or creative, athletic side while training. Examples might include challenging yourself to hit 'improvised shots' around, over or

under obstacles. Get into competitive practice games with friend. Use the same club to hit different shots, etc. Create practice situations where you have to react, not think.

10. **Separate mental practice from physical practice.** There are times in practice when you need to be very deliberate and thoughtful. Those are times when you're working on honing fundamentals or doing drills to capture a specific technique. Other times, you might be focusing on the athletic or completive side of the game— developing your pre-shot routing, tempo, visualization, feel, etc. Both are equally important, but don't try to work on them at the same time.

You might be asking yourself about now if your practice routine is even close to what it needs to be. If your practice doesn't require your full attention, if you rarely use a pre-shot routine, if you hit balls the same distance with the same club or stroke putts from the same distance over and over again and hit all your shots from good lies, you probably need to improve your practice approach. This kind of session is all too common (*ball-beating* is the slang term) and will make you only a pretty good practice range player but is no way to prepare you to be a polished competitive golfer. The goal of practice is to learn new skills, master them and, most importantly, transfer them to the golf course under competitive conditions. The best way to do that is to practice in a way that reflects how you play. A good practice isn't judged by how well you can hit a 7-iron off a perfect lie. A good practice means you focused on each shot; you simulated a live round in little ways, like switching clubs between shots, or hitting different yardages with the same club, or hit out of less-than-perfect lies and didn't turn to a coach after every shot but rather learned how to analyze your own performance. After all, there are no coaches on the 18th fairway when you need to make par to save a one-shot lead, are there?

Obviously all this hard work requires a significant commitment. But does it work? Does proper practice produce elite performance? Of this there is no guarantee. After all, an elephant can practice all it wants, it's never going to be a giraffe. "In sport, deliberate practice is often not enough to ensure success," notes Dr. Janet Starks, the chair of the department of kinesiology at McMaster University and a leading researcher in expert performance. "There are factors of character, of luck, of the environment and of avoiding injury that inevitably affect the outcome of competitions. These factors are one reason why sports are so interesting to perform and watch; you just never know." What *is* guaranteed is that, while deliberate practice won't automatically make you an elite golfer, failing to learn how to practice properly will ensure that you will never reach your ultimate playing potential, whatever that might be. There are many examples that prove the point.

But as an example of what deliberate practice *can* do, consider the recent rise to prominence of female golfers from South Korea. When Se Ri Pak burst onto the LPGA scene in 1998 by winning two major championships as a rookie on the way to a hall-of-fame career, the only thing as surprising as her game was her nationality. There were only five South Koreans on the LPGA Tour the season before Pak made her debut. Ten years later, there were 45 South Korean women playing on Tour while 33 played in the 2007 U.S. Women's Open, earning more than 20% of the 156 spots available. This despite taking up the game in a country the size of Indiana with less than 250 golf courses for 49 million people. And it's not like the South Korean climate is ideal for the game—it can be bitterly cold in winter and impossibly wet in summer. Pak estimates that the playing season lasts about two months a year. In any case, it's not like anyone can just get a tee time anyway—golf is expensive and many clubs are private.

So how to explain the rush to success in North America? One is the example Pak set. By winning two major championships weeks apart in 1998, Pak became a massive celebrity in South Korea inspiring a generation of South Korean girls to take up the sport. According to Dr. Ericsson's research, you could expect that it would a take a decade before the full impact was felt, as thousands of hopeful girls began working on their skills. Sure enough, the number of South Koreans on the LPGA jumped from five the year before Pak's rookie season to 45 in 2007. Strangely enough, part of the reason for their success may be because they have such a difficult time getting on a golf course. The lack of access means more time is spent on the multi-level driving ranges that dot the country, practicing with a focus on fundamentals.

"We grew up that way," Pak says. "The culture says that's the way you play golf. Here [in North America] you can [play] all the time because of the courses available. It's not that way in Korea." And all that focused work? It goes a long way to developing myelin—the magic that helps make champions.

PRACTICE AND THE STAGES OF DEVELOPMENT

Practice means different things at different stages of a player's development.

In studies concerning the development of elite athletes, renowned sports science researcher Dr. Jean Côté, Professor and

Director of the School of Kinesiology and Health Studies at Queen's University, found that there were clear patterns that emerged. He identified three stages of sport development from childhood to late adolescence as the Sampling Years (ages 6-12); the Specializing Years (ages 13-15); and the Investment Years (age 16 and up).

The Sampling, Specializing and Investment years are differentiated by, and based on, the amount of the participant's deliberate practice (structured formal training) and deliberate play (neighborhood play using the general rules of the game without being an organized league), i.e., pick-up basketball.

THE SAMPLING YEARS: AGES 6-12

The Sampling Years are characterized by a low frequency of deliberate practice and a high frequency of deliberate play. Simply, athletes in this stage develop most effectively when they are provided with the opportunity to play informal games for hundreds of hours (deliberate play). In these games and activities, the players can use their creativity to modify the rules of the sport to suit the situation. They require very little structured practice and drills (deliberate practice) led by coaches or parents.

Golf should be introduced to children who show interest in the sport when they are in the Sampling Years. It should be one of several activities that they explore. Ideally, children interested in the sport should participate in an organized golf skills development program that is fun and appealing. This program should be conducted by an individual trained in junior golf coaching. Children at this stage need to gain as much experience as possible by playing the game. They should be taught the basic fundamentals and then given the opportunity to play the sport. There should be little concern for competing in organized tournaments at this stage.

THE SPECIALIZING YEA

In the development of elite athlete:
point occurs at approximately age 13 v
secondary school. They reduce their involve
and begin to compete at the regional or nat.
primary sport.

The Specializing Years mark a transition in
gradually decrease their involvement in various ext
activities and focus on one or two sporting activiti
fun and excitement remained central elements of the s
experience, sport-specific development emerged as a characte
of the child's involvement.

The research suggests that if a child is passionate about golt,
and has the desire and aptitude to potentially advance as an elite
level player in golf, then at the age of about 13, he should make
golf one of his 'top two' sports. He should align himself with a
professional coach who is trained and specializes in developing
competitive players. He should develop peer group relationships
with other athletes who have the same interests. He should practice,
play and compete in the same fashion as other top aspiring high
performance athletes in all sports.

Elite golfers should follow periodized annual plans and be aware
of and respect the recommended practice-to-competition ratios.

In the specializing years, athletes need to shift to approximately
equal amounts of deliberate play and deliberate practice. They
need to learn effective practice habits and training regimens.

INVESTMENT YEARS: AGE 16 AND UP

As elite athletes continue to develop, another transition point
occurs at approximately age 16. This is when athletes make a

to be elite athletes and consequently invest most all of
isure time into training and competing.

this stage, the child becomes committed to achieving an
level of performance. These athletes are focused on their
sen sport and usually one or two additional off-season sports
activities.

If an athlete is committed to developing his skills as an elite
level golfer, he should make golf his primary sport by age 16. He
or she should train and compete in a professional fashion under
the guidance of a highly-trained golf coach who specializes in
player development. He or she should be enrolled in an Olympic-
type coaching, training and development program with other
like-minded athletes, if possible.

At this level, the golfer should invest the vast majority of his
free time to developing his skills as an aspiring elite level golfer. He
should be engaged in deliberate practice activities for three to five
hours per day in addition to competing and playing the game.

6

PLAYING YOUR BEST
WHEN YOU NEED TO MOST

IT WAS LATE IN THE AFTERNOON on one of the greatest
days in the history of golf. Tiger Woods was playing the final
nine holes at the 2000 U.S. Open at Pebble Beach Golf Links,
also known as "God's home course." The outcome was already
decided. Woods had started the round with a 10-shot lead over
playing partner Ernie Els, making the final 18 holes a coronation,
rather than a competition. It was an incredible start to what
would be an incredible summer. In addition to winning his first
U.S. Open championship, Woods went on to win the British Open
in record fashion at St. Andrews, and then out-lasted Bob May
in a thrilling final round showdown for the PGA Championship
at Valhalla to become the first golfer since Ben Hogan to win
three straight majors. But with the title virtually already decided,
Woods caught fire on Pebble's famous back-nine anyway. Leading
by nine shots and standing at eight-under-par (no one else broke
par for the tournament!) Woods birdied the 10th and followed
up with a birdie at the 12th to move to 10-under, becoming only
the second player in U.S. Open history to get that far into red
figures. He stiffed a sand wedge to a foot of the 13th and made an

eight-footer at the 15th to get to 12-under-par. No one in the then 100-year history of the U.S. Open had ever been that far under par. With a 15 shot lead, Woods was about to break a record for margin of victory at a major championship that was set by Old Tom Morris at the 1862 British Open (13 shots); a mark that had stood for 138 years!

Woods could have been forgiven for waltzing his way home from there—playing to the crowds; tipping his hat; playing the last three holes with a cue stick, even. But there he stood over a 15-foot par putt on the par 4 16th with brow furrowed, grinding like the championship itself was riding on this single putt. Sure enough the ball held its line over the late afternoon bumps and ridges and tumbled in just as he had envisioned, with Woods celebrating like he'd just made birdie to win his first professional tournament. Why? What could possibly have been such a big deal with one of golf's greatest championships already locked down, the trophy engraved, the cheque all but cashed, the history books already being rewritten?

"I knew if I went out there and made no bogeys, if I was patient, I knew I'd make a putt here and there and maybe increase the lead," said Woods. "...so that was one of the biggest moments of the day. I worked so hard not to make a bogey. If I had missed that putt, I would have been ticked at myself. I didn't want to make a bogey today."

And he didn't. He parred his way home, set records that perhaps only he will ever break and served notice—as subtly as the neon lights up the Las Vegas strip—that he was well on his way to becoming the greatest golfer of all time.

The applicable lesson for all the mortals watching, however, had nothing to do with stiffing wedges or carving fairways or leaving the best golfers in the world wondering if they were in the wrong line of work. The lesson is that, in order to play your best, you have to think your best. Woods wasn't standing on the first tee thinking about pushing his ball around in order to preserve his lead and win the U.S. Open. He was standing on the first tee beside Ernie Els, with one goal in mind—play a bogey-free round of golf. He wasn't thinking about the result (winning and setting records), he was setting an important intermediate and achievable goal of playing 18 holes without a bogey. That, in turn, forced him to stay in the moment (which explains why he was grinding on a relatively meaningless par putt) and required a commitment to the process of playing good golf (sticking with his routine, focusing on each shot alone and following a game plan). No one will ever lose an argument that Tiger Woods is the most physically talented golfer the sport has ever known. But the reason his talents are on display so obviously is that he may also be, quite possibly, the most mentally-gifted player the game has ever seen. It's a pretty good combination.

Chances are you're not the next Tiger Woods. No offense intended. He is a mature prodigy on par with historical geniuses in other fields, be it Mozart in music or Bobby Fischer in chess. He was born with a gift. His father recognized it and created an environment that helped it flourish, and Tiger himself used his passion for the game to find every possible way to reach his full potential. But there is much to learn from Tiger's example, and the best part is that some of the most important aspects of his game can be imitated by golfers who don't have his incredible physical ability. Even better? Learning to think like a champion is a skill that that you can use every day, even if you never set foot on a golf course. There are several elements involved, of course, but what follows are three main principles that will help your mental game on and off the course.

MAKE YOURSELF A TREE

If you've spent much time studying the golf swing, or at least being taught well, you've probably heard the truism that a solid foundation is the start of a solid swing. When you stand over the ball, you need to be in a balanced, athletic position starting from your feet on up. If your lower body is in a good fundamental position, it will be easier to build a powerful, repeatable swing. But to truly have a solid golf game, you need an approach to the game that starts, not from the ground up, but from below the ground. A mighty oak is the grandest of trees, but only because its root system runs nearly as deeply and broadly below the ground as its branches and leaves do above.

Oaks even have a special place in golf: there are hundreds of them on the property of Augusta National, site of the Masters. But one is more famous than all the others, as it stands just behind the club house and up the hill from the first tee and 18th green. As a result, it's the perfect place to meet before or after a round. During Master's week, it's *the* place to meet. Stand under the oak tree long enough and you'll see everyone who's anyone in the world of golf. It's where Tiger stops to greet old friends and where everyone from Arnold Palmer to Jack Nicklaus pauses to catch up on gossip.

The importance here is that if you have plans on being a serious player, you have to pay just as much attention to your fundamentals before you ever pick up a golf club. A tree has three main parts: The roots, the trunk and the branches. The branches are the last part of the tree to develop, and the most visible. That's where all the glory is—the low scores, the tournament wins, the recognition. The roots are where the foundation for all that success is built. Not everyone sees them, but they are vitally important. And the trunk is the part that joins the roots with the branches. For golfers to realize their goals, their roots have to be inline with the branches.

Thinking like a champion, in large part, means behaving like a champion. This is the part of the game that has very little to do with natural ability, and almost everything to do with your outlook, attitude and discipline. These are things you can control, and given the number of things you can't control in golf—winds, lies, funky bounces, just to name the big three—neglecting to give your best effort in the areas that are within your control is making a choice to fail.

If we're going to be mighty mental oaks as players, we have to start at the roots. Some examples of roots that need to be nurtured in a young sapling (junior player) are the fundamentals of technique. These include sound short game habits and a strong basic understanding of the golf swing. These are physical aspects of the game, but unless you embrace them with the proper mental outlook, your best golf will always elude you. Sure you practice, but do you practice correctly? Given all the time you invest in the game as a young player, it only makes sense that the time you spend is maximized and you develop practice routines and habits that will last a lifetime. This will help you through the inevitable slumps and be the backbone of the occasional triumph. And don't overlook the importance of healthy personal relationships with parents, peers and coaches, all of whom play a key role in you reaching your potential. They need to be counted on to be there in good times and bad. These 'roots' along with your equipment, mental preparation, and nutrition are things you can control to help you be the best you can be at any given moment.

Strong and deep roots help a tree withstand storms also known in golf as *slumps.* As long as the trunk (the golfer's goals)

THE TREE METAPHOR

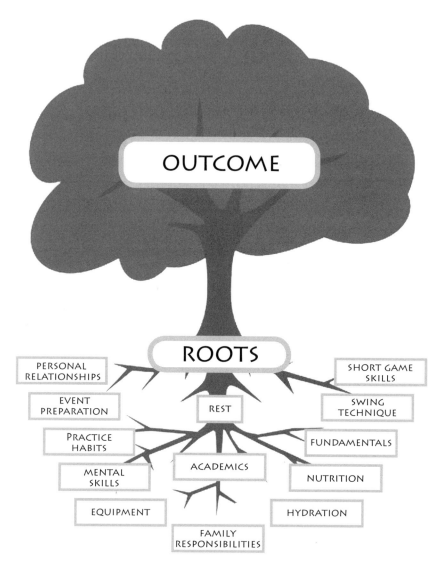

OUTCOME

ROOTS

PERSONAL RELATIONSHIPS

SHORT GAME SKILLS

EVENT PREPARATION

REST

SWING TECHNIQUE

PRACTICE HABITS

FUNDAMENTALS

MENTAL SKILLS

ACADEMICS

NUTRITION

EQUIPMENT

HYDRATION

FAMILY RESPONSIBILITIES

ONGOING FOCUS OF ATHLETE AND COACH

**DEVELOP STRONG AND DEEP ROOTS
TO GET IMPROVED RESULTS**

are inline with the roots, the tree will grow tall and the branches broad in due time. Like a tree growing, these things can't be rushed. Coaches and parents (the gardeners) need to listen and be attentive to the young saplings and be prepared to 'weed out' problems with appropriate discipline as they arise. With all these preconditions in place, your golf game can grow tall and strong. And what do the biggest oaks do? Their acorns fall, planting the seeds for other oaks to grow, nurturing a new generation of players. Tiger's roots run deep—his close relationship with his parents, his loyalty to a small group of old friends and his willingness to compete no matter what the circumstances—prove that. But perhaps the most important sign that he has become the mightiest oak in golf are all the young players he's inspired to take up the game.

BE A SELF MANAGER

When you boil it right down, reaching your potential in golf isn't all that far removed from becoming a well-developed person in other walks of life. Which is why pursuing your dreams in golf is worthwhile. The odds of anyone reading this book becoming the next Tiger Woods are astronomical. He is a special talent that comes along once every 50 years or so. The odds of anyone reading this book actually making the PGA Tour or the LPGA Tour are not quite as long, but let's face it, becoming one of the best 200 or so golfers in the world is an incredibly steep hill to climb. But if in striving for those goals you can learn to develop habits that serve you well in other aspects of life, it's a task that's well worth the effort.

With that in mind, perhaps there's no goal more worth undertaking than becoming your own self-manager. It's not always possible to be your own boss—and even bosses usually answer to someone. But we all have the opportunity to manage how we conduct ourselves no matter what we do in life. People who take on that role typically have a good chance of realizing their potential in golf or anything else.

What does it mean to be a self-manager? According to Dr. John Marshall, a psychologist who used his experience as a professional hockey player to further his expertise in the study of competition and motivation, self-managers are those who take responsibility for their path, set goals and commit to strategies to meet them. "Being managed means following directions," says Dr. Marshall, Founder and Chairman of the Self-Management Group. "Self-management means finding them."

Again, these are aspects of your golf growth that you can control. Marshall has identified nine principles of self management, and they are all directly transferable to the golf course.

1. **Performance.** The key to success. You are accountable for your results (your score, for example), but you are responsible for your performance (being prepared; maintaining a solid focus throughout your round).

2. **Expectations dictate performance.** If you think you can or think you can't—you're right!

3. **Reinforcement creates habits.** You only have to do it until you want to do it, then you don't have to do it any more.

4. **Motivate yourself, others can't.** 90% pull ("Mom, can you take me to practice?") and 10% pull ("Son, you better get ready for practice") is the ideal motivational mix.

5. **Maximizing your Return on Energy (ROE).** Do this by

a) deciding what you're going to commit to achieving, b) prioritizing what steps are required to achieve those goals, and c) spending the appropriate amount of energy to meet your priorities according to those commitments.

6. **Manage effort.** There is only one way to move from objectives to results—EFFORT!

7. **Manage self-confidence.** Expectations determine performance and it's self-confidence that determines expectations.

8. **Commit yourself.** Change "I should" to "I will" and set a timetable.

9. **Decide once.** Psychological time management—put your energy into doing it, not into thinking you should do it.

Practical applications? A golfer determined to succeed will take charge of the process. Golfers who reach plateaus and get stuck or who can't seem to quite harness their talent tend to be in a rut, repeating the same habits and strategies yet expecting a different result. According to Marshall, champions are those who use their self-management skills to identify their strengths and weaknesses and develop strategies to improve, gaining an edge over their competition. Rather than doing the same things that don't work, an equation Marshall describes as $1 \times 1 \times 1 \times 1 \times 1 = 1$, where the end result is the same as before; self-managers use a slightly different equation—think of it as $1.1 \times 1.1 \times 1.1 \times 1.1 =$ enhanced performance. The number of factors that are 1.1s are many and varied, but some obvious examples are: ensuring your equipment is optimally fitted; preparing written game plans; preparing a formal goal-setting plan; eating properly on and off the course; getting adequate rest and working with a professional coach. The result of these and many other small but significant steps are ways you can 'manage' your game and will result in your becoming a better player.

THINK LIKE A CHAMPION

There's an understandable tendency to look at players at the highest level and presume that they got there mostly because they have a rare amount of natural ability that others don't have, hence they become successful. And there's certainly some truth in that assumption. But that only makes professionals roughly as talented as most of the other players on the PGA Tour or LPGA Tour. So what is it among the best of the best that sets them apart? What allows some golfers to enjoy long, satisfying careers in professional golf while others come and go without ever being noticed? You can bet that those that reach their potential at the highest levels of golf not only have loads of physical talent, but a mental game that is every bit as impressive.

In their book *The 8 Traits of Champion Golfers*, Dr. Deborah Graham and Jon Stabler of GolfPsych drew on their experience studying and working with some of the best golfers in the world to summarize just what it was that set them apart from their peers. And while everyone is a little different, Graham and Stabler learned that champions share eight mental traits that allowed them to perform their best. What are they, you ask? Excellent question. Working with everyone from Tom Kite to Greg Norman to Brandie Burton, Graham and Stabler learned that champions typically had:

1. **Good focus.** A good mental routine for each shot with a narrow focus on the target. A wider focus

(alert, but not so locked in that they couldn't chat with their partner or notice the weather) between shots but, in general, were not easily distracted from the task at hand.

2. **Abstract thinking.** While playing, they focus on course management and relevant variables only (What kind of lie do I have? Which direction is the wind coming from?), rather than wasting energy on over-thinking or over-analyzing (Am I sure this is the right club? What club is my playing partner using? How many shots over par am I?)

3. **Emotionally stable.** Poor shots or bad breaks get roughly the same reaction as good shots or good breaks— regardless of the outcome, the focus shifts quickly to the next shot or next situation, leaving little time to mope, celebrate or be angry, recognizing the next shot is just as important as the last.

4. **Dominant.** Plays with controlled aggression, willing to take smart risks and challenge the golf course when the opportunity presents itself.

5. **Tough-minded.** Self-reliant; indifferent to the opinions of other competitors; overcomes adversity and unaffected by adverse conditions. Respects his opponents, but understands that the goal is to beat them.

6. **Confident.** Secure, self-satisfied and guilt free. They see themselves as winners because they've taken the necessary steps to earn their success.

7. **Self-sufficient.** Very decisive and prefer their own decisions, yet still open to useful input from coaches, caddies or those close to them. Resistant to peer pressure.

8. **Optimum Arousal.** Aware of and control their level of tension to enhance performance. On a 1-to-10 scale, four for putting, six for driving. They come to the golf course excited, enthusiastic and prepared to overcome whatever challenges the round brings, but not so stimulated that their mind and body becomes tense, their nerves overcoming them physically and mentally.

As with the physical side of the game, some individuals come by these traits more easily than others. And as with the physical side of the game, these traits can be improved with practice and strategies that help you develop where you need it (learning how to make your pre-round nerves work for you in a positive way) and maintain your strengths (making sure your willingness to improve is channeled in the most beneficial ways).

That's big picture stuff that even the best golfers work on throughout their careers. But improving your mental game can make a significant difference in a given round as soon as tomorrow. Imagine a scenario where you've missed badly with a club and a yardage you're normally quite comfortable with. What happens next can dictate what happens over the next three or four holes, if not the entire round. After a poor shot, most players instantly begin analyzing their mechanics, automatically engaging the right side of their brain, which is fine if you're trying to solve a math problem, but an obstacle if you're trying to remain in the calm, flowing state that is the ideal for competitive golf. Suddenly swing thoughts are coming hard and fast and the next shot is no better than the first. Did you hear that whistle? That's the bogey train leaving the station.

With the right mental approach, you can accept a bad shot for what it likely is—a bad shot—and get on with the task of putting the ball in the hole. The people at GolfPsych recommend pausing after a bad shot and asking yourself four simple questions—try it the next time you hit a bad shot.

1. **How was my tempo and rhythm?** If it was too slow or too quick, then the goal for the next shot or putt is simply to have better tempo or rhythm.
2. **How was my commitment to my club, target or type of shot?** If you were having second thoughts, the goal for the next shot or putt is to be totally committed to whatever choice you make.
3. **How was my visualization?** If the answer is you didn't take the time in your routine, or that you couldn't see the shot as well as you would like, then the goal is to visualize very well on your next shot or putt.
4. **How was my feel?** If the answer is, "I didn't feel the shot" or "I skipped the feel step," then the goal is to emphasize feel during your next routine.

Since it is widely accepted that over 90% of all poor shots for low handicap players are the result of mental mistakes that lead to physical mistakes, it only makes sense to examine the mental side of your game to find a solution for a shot that was less than ideal. An added benefit is that emphasizing the mental game utilizes the right side of your brain, which is where you need to be when you're playing your best golf. It will help you isolate the nature of the problem sooner and give you a better chance at preventing a series of bad shots or bad holes. By getting your round back on track, the chance of your emotions getting the better of you diminishes and what could be a poor round has a chance to become a good one.

This is but one example of how developing your mental skills can pay dividends. Another is the development of a solid pre-shot routine. A good pre-shot mental routine is simple and easy to repeat under pressure, encourages you to react to a target and helps you focus on playing golf instead of 'golf swing.' A good pre-shot mental routine gets rid of all the clutter of thoughts that can creep in if you don't train your thought process properly. Similarly, just as there are certain physical fundamentals included in a good putting stroke, there are things you can do mentally that will help you roll the rock well too, including being able to 'see' the ball roll on your intended line and 'hear' it fall into the hole during practice strokes. These are just some of the critical mental skills—call them brain fundamentals—that you need to practice just as you need to spend time making sure your grip, stance, posture and alignment are sound as well. The people at GolfPsych even have a mental game questionnaire you can take that will help you determine your mental game handicap. Once you know your strengths and weaknesses in these areas, you can work to improve them right along with your long game and your chipping and putting.

And improvement is the name of the game. Back at Pebble Beach in 2000, with his record-setting U.S. Open win in his pocket, Tiger Woods credited his incredible week—one that quite possibly surpassed even his mind-blowing 1997 Masters win during his professional debut there—not to great driving or amazing putting. Instead it was his mental game that made the difference. "I've had two great weeks in major championships," said Woods. "There comes a point where you feel tranquil, calm and at ease with yourself. Things just flowed. No matter what you do good or bad, it doesn't get to you. And to have those weeks coincide with majors is even better."

But Woods wasn't content to rest on his accomplishments, as amazing as they were at the time. Perhaps the most important of his mental gifts is that he enjoys his success, but his drive to improve never seems to change. "I can tell you one thing," Woods said, moments after finishing what many people think is the best four rounds of golf ever played. "And this is something I've said before and I will continue to say: I'm going to try to get better. You're always trying to work on things in this game, trying to get a little bit better."

7

STRONG IN BODY:
FITNESS AND NUTRITION FOR GOLF

AL GEIBERGER MAY NOT BE A HOUSEHOLD NAME in golf
these days, or at least among younger golfers. But he's a name
worth knowing for plenty of good reasons. Some long-time Tour
watchers will tell you his ball-striking was in the league of greats
like Ben Hogan and Lee Trevino. He's most often remembered
as Mr. 59. The lanky Californian with the sweet swing became
the first player in the history of the PGA Tour to break 60 when
he logged a 13-under-par round on June 10, 1977 at 7,249-yard
Colonial Country Club in Memphis in the PGA Tour's Danny
Thomas Memphis Classic, which he went on to win. Only two
PGA Tour players (Chip Beck and David Duval) and one LPGA
Tour member (Annika Sorenstam) have broken 60 since, and no
one has shot a round better than Geiberger's. He's an 11-time
winner on the PGA Tour, including a major champion, and he's
won 10 times on the Champions Tour. When his son Brent won
the Chrysler Classic of Greensboro in 2004, as his dad did in
1976, the pair became the first father-and-son duo to have won
the same PGA Tour event. All of which makes Geiberger part of
the game's essential fabric, and a character serious golfers should
know about. But that's not why they call him Skippy.

So thin that he long carried the nickname 'Bones,' since he was a teenager, Geiberger had developed the habit of nibbling snacks during his golf rounds. It turns out he has low blood sugar, and he was merely taking a common sense approach to keeping his focus at a high level during a long round of golf. At the 1965 PGA Championship, Geiberger was playing in a high-profile pairing with Arnold Palmer at The King's home course, Laurel Valley Country Club, in Ligonier, Pennsylvania. Surrounded by Arnie's Army, Geiberger knew he would never be able to slip off to the concession stands to grab a bite to eat. But that morning he saw his wife Judy making a peanut butter and jelly sandwich for their daughter Lee Ann, and took a couple with him for his round. "It worked out super," he said years later. "Whenever I needed a lift, I simply went to my bag and got a sandwich." Reporters noticed, and a month later when Geiberger won the American Golf Classic at Firestone Country Club, the peanut butter sandwiches become a fun piece of colour for reporters' stories. A year later the 1966 PGA Championship was at Firestone and it became more than a fun sidebar. Geiberger was playing some of the best golf of his life and entered the final round with a four-shot lead, but was on the verge of blowing it with bogeys on the three of the first four holes to start the final round. As if scripted, Geiberger reached into his bag for a sandwich, birdied the fifth and never looked back as he won his only major championship by four shots. It was the peanut butter sandwich heard 'round the golf world, and even earned Geiberger an endorsement deal with Skippy peanut butter, not to mention a nickname for life.

Geiberger was only doing what came naturally. He knew that his golf suffered when he got hungry while playing. And he stumbled on a peanut butter and jam sandwich as the perfect meal replacement—it combined proteins and carbohydrates and was easy to carry in a golf bag and nibble between shots. But it was a story because, at the time, sports nutrition was still in the Dark Ages, as were the principles of fitness in general. Kids growing up in the 1970s, when Geiberger was playing his best golf, were still being told in gym classes not to swallow water during breaks. Instead the advice was to merely rinse out your dry mouth and spit out the rest for fear of cramping. Chocolate bars and other sugary snacks were thought to be good food for aspiring athletes, the quick carbohydrate rush confused with a useful energy boost, despite the inevitable sugar crashes that followed. If anything, golf was behind even that level of enlightenment.

Walter Hagen is revered as one of the sport's all-time greats, trailing only Jack Nicklaus and Tiger Woods for the number of major championship titles won during his career. But Hagen became a star, not only because he won every tournament in sight, but because he managed to do it while living an apparent life of excess including occasionally showing up for his tee-time still dressed in top hat and tails from the night before. The great Ben Hogan and Palmer were both fierce smokers on the golf course. And Gary Player, the wiry South African star, was thought a bit kooky when he let on how big a part his commitment to physical fitness—he works outs for 90 minutes a day, five days a week even now, in his 70s—played in his remarkable career, which earned him 163 wins worldwide, as well as nine major titles.

Things change, however, even golf. As fitness became a bigger part of everyday lifestyles in the 1980s and 1990s, golfers took note. As with most things in the game these days, Tiger Woods has set the bar. The whip skinny teenager who broke into professional golf in 1996 has steadily gained muscle throughout his professional career thanks to a strength-training program that he has always kept a closely guarded secret. The results were never more obvious than when he won his 13th major title at the 2007 PGA Championship at Southern Hills Country Club in Tulsa, Oklahoma. He dropped a 35-foot birdie putt from just off the green and greeted it with one of his trademark violent fist pumps. With his shirt soaked with his own sweat thanks to the 100-degree heat, it was clear that had Woods ever connected with anything other than air he was in good condition to deliver a considerable blow, his physique now resembling that of a National Football League free safety.

But perhaps more significant than his broad shoulders or lean stomach is the fact that Woods' attention to strength building as part of his golf routine allowed him to develop his famous 'stinger'—a low-screaming tee shot that he hits with great control thanks in part to his powerful wrists and forearms. They allow him to hold the clubface slightly closed through impact, a requirement for the difficult, yet useful shot. If Woods would ever allow his secrets to become public, his image as the perfect modern golfer would be complete. If his impeccable game is built on a foundation of strength training, flexibility, endurance and nutrition, shouldn't yours?

Strength Training for Golf

While the notion of resistance training and golf isn't as foreign now as it might have been when Al Geiberger was firing his round of 59—his nickname before Skippy was Bones, remember—it's still true that simply doing any kind of weight training won't automatically help and may even hurt a golfer's development. When football players are in the weight room, their plan is to develop power and explosiveness through the biggest muscle groups—the thighs, chest, arms and back. In a sense, they're trying to add armor to themselves. Golfers don't have to worry about getting hit by fast-moving, angry people. And a packed chest and beach biceps don't do much for you when you're trying to feather an easy sand wedge off a tight lie over water.

So hitting the weight room and knocking off a few preacher curls or other traditional body-building exercises isn't the answer. There are two reasons for this. The first is that the essence of a successful golf swing is that an amazingly broad range of muscle groups need to be coordinated and fire in a perfectly-timed sequence to produce a smooth, flowing and balanced pass at the ball. Think about it. The great golf swings in history aren't wild, powerful wood chops; the swings most people find most enviable seem to happen nearly in slow motion, like the golfer is barely trying. At 6-foot-4 and 220 pounds, Vijay Singh is an imposing physical presence. He could do some damage to a tree with an axe in his hands, no doubt. But his swing looks like he's got motor oil in his joints: there are no signs of friction, even though Singh is one of the most dedicated players on Tour in terms of strength training. The second problem with merely trying to add mass in the weight room is that a good golf swing requires the muscles to support the joints at proper angles. Adding too much size in one area compared with another can actually throw off the angles that make your swing work, and your performance may suffer, even if you do look better in a T-shirt.

The key is getting stronger the right way. For golf purposes this means using strength training to support the correct muscles firing at the optimum time with the correct joint angles to form the foundation of a solid swing. Done the right way, the golfer can expect to develop a more powerful, consistent swing. But that's only part of the strength training equation.

Just as important is injury prevention and skill development. For every shot hit in a competitive round, thousands are taken in a practice environment. But if you're hurt or simply nursing nagging pain in areas that are quite common to golf—lower back, neck, shoulder, wrist and hands—you can't practice with the vigour and intensity required, and it never takes long for a disruption in your practice routine to creep into your game.

Improved strength and fitness can even help in areas of the game where strength seems least important. What could being stronger have to do with making four-foot putts? But one of the keys to making four-foot putts is practicing them. A well-conditioned lower-back and abdomen can be the difference between comfortably standing over 100 four-footers in a drill (one of Phil Mickelson's favorite pre-round routines) and cutting short your putting practice or altering your posture as you get tired. Similarly if your stabilizer and postural muscles are fit and well-conditioned, you can not only develop more power with your full swings, you can maintain the angles needed to make those swings work even as fatigue begins to creep in at the end of a long practice session or on the walk to the 18th tee on a hot day.

The benefits of strength training are many, but there are still myths associated with the practice that should be put to rest:

1. **Strength training for performance is the same as training for fitness.** As we suggested above, this is a mistake. Your buddies might head to the weight room to add some size to their arms but you are there as one part of an overall training regimen to improve your golf performance. The goal is building

movement specific strength, not looking good at the beach.

2. **Strength training will automatically add muscle mass.** Not true. The performance of the muscle can be improved without adding size.

3. **No pain, no gain.** This is a popular expression, but it doesn't always bear out when training properly. Since the goal is to be stronger, not bigger, pushing the muscles to failure and the burning sensation that comes with it ('the pain') isn't the way to go. Instead, focusing on proper technique with a long-term, planned approach will improve the function of the muscles required for your game.

4. **My trainer should be stacked.** Just because your trainer looks like he can lift the rear end of a car, doesn't mean he's the right person to improve your golf fitness. Find someone with a background in exercise physiology (the science of exercise) who has Titleist Performance Institute (TPI) golf specific training and certification. Log onto www.mytpi.com to see individuals in your area with this expertise. Find someone who can design specific training strategies to help you excel. They should be evaluated based on what they know, not how fit they might look.

5. **Strength training is for the off-season.** Wrong again. Whatever advances made during the non-competitive parts of the year will be lost if a strength training program isn't followed year round.

FLEXIBILITY TRAINING FOR GOLF

Strength training is only one component of a complete approach to golf fitness. One of the most overlooked areas is flexibility. One reason is it's just not something most players get a lot of satisfaction from doing. The benefits aren't always obvious but, rest assured, they are there.

The key is to identify stretching routines and techniques that impact on the golf swing specifically. Like strength training, proper stretching can add power to your game by improving your range of motion and, just as important, it can help you prevent injury.

There are two primary methods for training flexibility in the areas golfers typically need it most—shoulders, hips, lower back, abdominals and arms:

1. **Static Flexibility.** This is the type of stretching routine most people are automatically familiar with, and the kind of flexibility work done in nearly all sports as part of the warm-up and cool down. It involves slowly moving a joint to the stretched position; holding that position for 10 or 20 seconds, or until tension releases; relaxing the stretched muscle and then restretching. It's a safe, simple and low-risk way to improve or maintain your flexibility.

2. **Ballistic (Dynamic) Flexibility.** This involves training the muscles and joints to move freely even at the high rates of speed involved in a golf swing. There are two stages to ballistic flexibility training: a. the warm-up, where you progressively rotate the upper body, arms and hips with increasing intensity in movements that exactly mirror the movement produced during the golf swing, and b. after the warm-up, these movements are repeated at maximum intensity for a pre-planned number of sets and repetitions based on your training readiness and experience. In other words, ballistic

flexibility is an advanced form of training that should be done under the supervision of a qualified exercise physiologist.

Why is flexibility important? Consider that one of the most significant differences between elite players and the rest is that top golfers have a greater range of motion throughout all stages of their golf swings, in particular through their lower back, upper back, shoulders and hips. As a result, regardless of other factors, elite players will have better and more powerful swings simply because they can get their club to different (and more desirable) angles than other players. If you want to be an elite player, you have to train your body to achieve a comparable range of motion. This might come more easily to some than others, but it's a step that can't be skipped by anyone with big dreams. So learn how to stretch, develop a good routine and do it regularly. You won't regret it. The benefits are considerable:

1. **Flexibility and injury prevention.** Stretching before training is, surprisingly, not the most important time to get loose, as the relationship between stretching and lower rates of injury is unclear. Stretching after training has been proven to reduce injuries, however. Also, because golf is an asymmetrical sport (i.e., you play right-handed or left-handed, but not both) it's important to maintain the same levels of flexibility on each side of your body. Failing to maintain that balance can lead to injuries. Similarly, the goal of a stretching program is to improve the flexibility in joints that are inflexible. If you already have good

flexibility in a joint and make it more flexible, the joint may became less stable and contribute to an injury.

2. **Flexibility and power.** The more flexible you are in the right places the better range of motion you have. Combined with proper technique, this can translate into increased clubhead speed and longer driving distances.

3. **Flexibility and training progression.** Just like it's not a good idea to head to the range and hit 200 practice balls if you haven't touched a club for three months, or start trying to set personal bests in the weight room when you haven't been lifting regularly, a stretching program requires a smooth build-up and progression to be most effective. Some basic guidelines:

   • Static stretching is a constant and should begin immediately and be included as part of the warm up and cool down of each training session.

   • Hold each stretch for about 60 seconds total, in either four sets of 15 seconds or three sets of 20 seconds, three to six days a week.

   • Ballistic stretching should only be started when you have the proper strength base and training experience.

   • The amount (volume) of ballistic stretching depends on your training experience.

   • Ballistic training should be done two days a week, with three or four days rest between sessions.

There are some common myths about flexibility training that are worth addressing as well, including:

1. **Is static stretching the only way to improve flexibility?** No. Static stretching is a great place to start a flexibility routine. But due to the ballistic nature of golf, dynamic flexibility must be progressively implemented over time as part of a golf specific flexibility program.

2. **Does stretching before playing prevent injuries?** Not necessarily. Stretching before playing improves your range of motion and is a helpful part of any warm-up. But stretching after playing has been shown to be a better way to prevent injuries.

3. **Does ballistic stretching lead to more injuries?** It can. Ballistic stretching is not for the inexperienced. Done too soon in a golfer's development or too often or without proper instruction, there is a chance of injury. Done properly and progressively, ballistic stretching reduces the chances of injury.

4. **Is a tight muscle a strong muscle?** No. A tight muscle is a weak muscle. Muscles that feel tight must be loosened through flexibility training or sports specific rehabilitation to allow greater range of motion in the golf swing.

5. **Which helps you hit the ball farther, improved strength or flexibility?** Golf-specific strength is important, but unless all the various muscle groups in the golf swing are flexible, they won't move in the smooth, co-ordinated manner that marks an elite golf swing.

6. **Do I have to stretch all season?** Of course. Flexibility is gained through progressive training. Stopping your stretching program means gains will be lost and your swing mechanics will suffer.

ENDURANCE TRAINING FOR GOLF

Let's face it. Some athletes prefer golf to other sports because they don't have to run. This is fine. No one is suggesting that golf requires the fitness of a soccer player. But ignore your aerobic condition at your peril. During an average round of golf you're on your feet for as much as six hours when you include the pre-round warm-up. It's not unusual for a golf course to measure 7,000 yards—and that's from tee to green. If you add in all the walking you do to line-up putts, looking for your or your partner's ball and measure of yardage, it's not uncommon to walk twice that distance during a round. Carrying your own bag adds to the demand. And don't forget that, most importantly, golf is played in the summer months when the temperature is highest and the demands on your fitness are most extreme.

While aerobic or endurance conditioning in other sports is necessary to compete at nearly any level, in golf, endurance conditioning is a complimentary aspect of your overall training that simply makes you more efficient in competition. While being fit doesn't guarantee that you'll make every putt, being out of shape is an invitation to tire as a round or tournament or season wears on, and tired golfers make mistakes, including missing makeable putts. And have you ever noticed those big putts seem to come when the green is at the top of a steep hill? A fit golfer will recover faster and settle down over the putt sooner.

Golfers become fatigued the same way other athletes become tired. As they exert themselves, they accumulate lactic acid—that's the burning feeling you get in your muscles when you work hard. As lactic acid accumulates, your swing mechanics will suffer. Just as important, as you get tired, your decision making suffers.

You're more likely to make a mistake with your yardages, misread a putt or simply lose your focus. As your muscles become less efficient, you begin to compensate in your swing and your chances of injury increase.

Fortunately, all of this can easily be fixed. Thirty minutes of aerobic training three-to-five days a week during the off-season and once or twice a week during the golf season is enough to provide the endurance required to play your best golf. Mixing in some increased intensity, such as interval training, can help you make considerable gains in fitness, but is best done under the supervision of an exercise physiologist. The results can not only off-set the problems caused by a lack of aerobic conditioning, but can provide benefits that poorly conditioned golfers don't experience: Your body gets better at clearing lactic acid; you don't get as tired during training and can practice longer and more effectively; your swing mechanics are maintained and your mental focus stays on your golf game, not on how hot it is. Taken together, your chances of playing good golf increase with your endurance.

Myths About Endurance Training for Golf

1. **Should I use those heart rate formulas to determine my aerobic fitness?** No. Those aren't very precise. It's preferable to get your aerobic fitness tested by an experienced trainer and base your endurance program on those findings.

2. **Isn't playing golf enough to get me in shape?** Yes, to a point. If you do nothing other than play golf, you will only be prepared for the challenges of a normal round

of golf. If you are playing extra holes or on a hilly course or playing in extreme heat, you will become tired. By including endurance training in your routine, you will be prepared for conditions that are more challenging than what is typical.

3. **Don't you need to train at a high intensity to gain any benefit from endurance training?** No. Nearly all your endurance work should be done at a 'base training' level according to your specific fitness. For some, that might mean a brisk walk; others a slow jog; for some, a fast run.

4. **Can aerobic training interfere with my practice?** Only if you do it incorrectly. If you do all your aerobic work at high intensity, you will end up over tired and it could affect your practice and play. Training at base intensity with some high intensity work will compliment your practice routine.

5. **Once the season starts, does the running stop?** No. You develop most of your aerobic base during the off-season, but if you don't maintain it during the competitive season, you will lose the gains you've made.

NUTRITION AND HYDRATION FOR GOLF

If you picture your overall golf fitness regimen as a three-legged stool, with strength, flexibility and endurance training each forming one leg, you could make the case that nutrition and hydration are the seat of the chair, the part that brings it all together and gives the legs their purpose. As Al Geiberger learned way back when he started downing those peanut butter and jam sandwiches, a five-hour round of golf can turn on some timely eating. Years later Geiberger would joke that it was he that brought golf into the modern era of sports nutrition, where players eat precise mixes of proteins and carbohydrates and drink specially designed sports drinks—along with plenty of water—to keep the whole system running. "See, I was a groundbreaker, ahead of my time, bringing science to golf," Geiberger says.

He wasn't. He was just doing what came naturally. But science and a good dose of common sense are now as much an important part of serious golf as properly fitted clubs. All the strength training, flexibility routines and endurance work in the world will do you little good if you get an energy crash late in your round because you haven't eaten enough or you opted for simple sugars instead of foods that provide more sustained energy. And what could be simpler that making sure you drink enough fluids— primarily water—during a hot day on the course? Eating well and drinking properly allows your mind and body to perform at their best in all conditions, and your scores will reflect it.

Nutritionist Joanne Flynn has helpfully broken down guidelines about healthy eating and drinking for golf into nine useful principles she calls the 'The Front Nine of Fit.'

Hole 1: Don't bogey breakfast. An ideal breakfast includes a mix of proteins (yogurt, skim milk, eggs, peanut butter) and complex carbohydrates (whole grain toast, whole grain cereals, fruit). A proper breakfast helps you regulate your blood sugar during the rest of the day.

Hole 2: Tea it up. Make the cut, eliminate coffee, caffeinated soda and 'energy' drinks. They inspire carbohydrate and sugar cravings, which are followed by low energy and lack of focus after the rush is gone. Choose green tea for its vitamin C, anti-cancer and weight loss properties.

Hole 3: Don't slice it…white bread that is! Switch from white bread (heavy in simple carbohydrates, much like sugar) to whole grain bread, which is rich in complex carbohydrates and digests more slowly, providing a steady release of energy.

Hole 4: The Power of Protein. Protein-rich foods (lean meats, chicken, turkey, fish, eggs, nuts, seeds, peanuts, beans) improve muscle mass, concentration, immunity and energy.

Hole 5: Junk food handicap. Packed with refined carbs (sugar) and saturated and trans fats, junk food tastes good, but the result is low energy, impaired focus, weight gain and poor athletic performance.

Hole 6: The 'Shark' says…Eat salmon. Salmon and other fish are rich in Omega-3 fatty acids that help brain and heart function. Seeds, nuts and eggs are also good.

Hole 7: Eat your 'greens.' Foods like spinach, kale and broccoli are rich in vitamins, minerals and fiber.

Hole 8: Eat on par…What to carry in the bag. Turn away from junk food. Bring your own almonds, walnuts, berries, seeds, low-sugar protein bars, low-fat cheese and water.

Hole 9: Don't become a 'water hazard.' Avoid sugary sports drinks. Water's benefits include fat metabolism, proper muscle and skin tone and energy. Try to drink a minimum 10 glasses of water per day.

Eating properly for competition doesn't happen by accident. Just as playing a good round of golf includes laying out a game plan and following it, eating and drinking properly do too. Gulping down a cola, fast-food burger and fries before your round because you didn't have time or more nutritious options weren't available merely reflects poor planning. Choosing a can of soda over water reflects poor discipline. A lack of planning and absence of discipline rarely result in top performances.

A competitive round of golf is not a casual walk or a brief workout. From warm-up to cool down, you're likely looking at a minimum of six hours, quite likely seven or more. During that time, you need your brain sharp and your body strong. Eating properly and drinking enough is crucial to both those objectives. And lurching from chocolate bar to chips to soft drinks to sports drinks merely results in your blood sugar levels spiking and falling, and your concentration following suit. The goal is to feel on your game all day.

The first step, and likely the simplest, is proper hydration. Because golf isn't as strenuous as basketball, hockey or running, the need to replace fluids isn't as obvious. But it's easy to lose as much as 2% of your total body weight in water and accompanying minerals and electrolytes through perspiration and respiration on a hot summer day. It's a simple problem to avoid. The goal should be to weigh the same before and after exercise. If you weigh 150 pounds and lost five pounds of water during the course of a round, you need to drink 20 to 24 ounces of fluids to regain the lost water. A golfer in this situation would be considered mildly dehydrated or worse. If you've ever finished a day of golf with a flushed, red face, bottomless thirst, dry warm skin, able to manage only small amounts of dark yellow urine, muscle cramping and headaches, congratulations, you know what it's like to be dehydrated. Chances are your day on the course featured poor concentration, a sloppy mental routine, poor decision making and a generally bad attitude. And chances are your performance reflected your state of mind. If all of this could be avoided by simply drinking early and often, why wouldn't you do it? Drink water before, during and following play.

If your urine is clear, you're properly hydrated. Drink something on every hole, but keep in mind your stomach appreciates small, regular drinks rather than large, infrequent gulps. In the heat of summer, it's important to be aware of replacing your electrolytes, which are lost during heavy sweating.

Even if you're drinking water regularly, if you haven't replaced your electrolytes you can still be dehydrated as your cells, tissues and organs can't function properly without a proper electrolyte balance. Popular sports drinks like Gatorade help in this respect, but are more sugary than they need to be. You can dilute them with water and get the same benefit or you can buy electrolyte drinks at a health food store and not worry about diluting them.

The second key step to feeling your best on the golf course is a solid pre-round meal. As always, you want a balance of slow release carbohydrates and protein—a breakfast of eggs and whole wheat toast instead of pancakes with syrup and orange juice, for example; or a tuna sandwich on whole wheat instead of a hot dog and fries at lunch. If you don't have the time, food or appetite to eat a proper meal before an early morning tee-time, plan ahead and bring an easy-to-mix protein shake. This is also a good solution for golfers who have a hard time eating because of a nervous stomach before a round. And eating doesn't stop once you hit your first tee shot. A golf bag should include a pocket full of nutritious snacks, ranging from nuts to fruit to sports bars, and yes, peanut butter sandwiches.

YEAR-ROUND GOLF CONDITIONING

The top professional golfers of the modern era are extremely strong, flexible and fit. They are willing to work out year round to maintain their 'fitness advantage.' To get the most out of your game, you need to know how to arrange your year-round workout schedule to maximize your results.

The experts at the Titleist Performance Institute have identified seven physical performance factors that are crucial to every golf conditioning program: posture, balance, mobility, stability (the combination of strength and balance), power, coordination and endurance.

These factors are interactive. For example, if you have poor posture, it will be difficult to have good balance. Likewise, mobility and stability are co-dependent; you cannot gain advantage from one in the absence of the other. A third example is the inter-relationship of power and coordination. It is almost impossible to produce maximum power without optimal coordination.

While you must pay attention to each of the seven physical performance factors, it is wise to emphasize certain ones at different times of the year.

You should split your calendar year into three phases:

Off-Season: 3 to 4 months (i.e., November to February)
Pre-Season: 1 to 2 months (i.e., March to April)
In-Season: 5 to 6 months (i.e., May to October)

Important: Even golfers who live in warm weather climates (such as San Diego or Phoenix) should divide their year into these three categories. Golf conditioning works best when there is a specific focus according to the time of year. Even if you can play golf year-round in your home environment, you will benefit from dividing your workouts into these types of segments.

There are several ways to divide up your year. Here is one of the best:

Off-Season Segment (Posture, Balance, Stability). Posture is perhaps the most crucial component of golf conditioning. It's not the most glamorous, but it's so important that it merits constant attention. Without good posture in your everyday life and in your golf address position, you cannot hope to maximize the other physical performance factors. Off-season is the perfect time to get as strong as possible. Weight training and the use of a stability ball will be your main tools. Don't be afraid to hit the weights hard and heavy—the stronger you can get, the better. This is also the best time to improve your balance because stability is the combination of strength and balance.

Pre-Season Segment (Power and Coordination). Pre-season is optimal for development of power. Power is strength at high speed. Since you have spent the off-season getting as strong as possible, this is the perfect time for power training. And since power is dependent upon good coordination, pre-season is also optimal for giving coordination drills a high priority in your workout.

In-Season Segment (Mobility and Endurance). During your actual golf season, you want to avoid any feeling of being 'muscle-bound' or unduly muscularly fatigued. Working on mobility, flexibility and endurance will keep you in fine shape and won't interfere with your swing motion. Thus, the in-season segment is perfect for stretching and cardio.

Source: Titleist Performance Institute

8

PLANNING TO WIN

WITHOUT EVEN KNOWING IT, Jack Nicklaus had a tremendous advantage when he was growing up. His home course, Scioto Golf Club in Columbus, Ohio had a great reverence for Bobby Jones, the legendary amateur and founder of Augusta National Golf Club, home of the Masters. It was at Scioto that Jones won the 1926 U.S. Open. It followed on the heels of Jones' win at the British Open that year, and made him the first golfer to win the two biggest events in the game in the same season. He also attended the 1931 Ryder Cup matches held at the club.

As a result, the image of Jones was everywhere around Scioto when a young Nicklaus, age 10, was brought there by his father to begin lessons with Jack Grout, who became Nicklaus's lifelong teacher. There was a photo of Jones in the locker room and another in the golf shop. Many members were avid fans of Jones and could recite details about his playing style, manners, as well as his remarkable career. There was little surprise that Jones became Nicklaus's first golf hero. In his autobiography, Nicklaus describes what Jones' influence meant to him:

"Practically from the time that I took up the game, I knew one golf statistic cold: Bob Jones had won 13 major championships over an eight-year span. It was made clear early to me…why this was such a prodigious achievement. To win one of the traditional championships, a man has to be a truly wonderful golfer, since they are held on much more testing courses than the general run of tournaments. Along with this, he has to be an equally outstanding competitor. With the whole field keyed up for big events, the tension is fierce and the pressure on the leaders becomes so nerve-wracking that in countless championships it has proved too much for seasoned golfers with reasonably good temperaments. The essence of Jones' greatness was that he could play great golf on the great occasions."

The Jones influence was obvious if you look at Nicklaus's record. In 1964, his third year on the PGA Tour, Nicklaus was the leading money winner, counting $113,000 in earnings. But he did not have, by his admission, "a truly successful season." He was happier with his year in 1963, when he finished second on the money list to Arnold Palmer. The reason? In 1963 Nicklaus won two majors, the Masters and The PGA Championship, while in 1964 he didn't win any.

The gap partially explained what happened in Nicklaus's career going forward. Already a three-time major winner, Nicklaus began to plan his increasingly busy schedule around the four biggest events in golf. In broad strokes, the formula called for him to take the week off prior to a major to allow him time to visit and practice with Grout. For the Masters, he would play four practice rounds at Augusta the week before, take a few days off and then return. For the U.S. Open and PGA Championship, he would try to visit the course weeks or months before to makes sure he understood its intricacies and the shots he would need to work on. For the British Open, he would head over 10 days or more before to get adjusted to the time change and the nuances of links golf. And while other golfers might have tried to fool themselves into thinking that a major championship was just another tournament, Nicklaus never bothered.

"My approach was always to try to peak for the major championships," he said. "Play as much golf as I thought I needed and that would put my game in the right shape. I used to try not to take a major in stride and make it like something else. I always put major tournaments up here [raising a hand above his head]. But I believed I could raise my game. You have to believe it to be able to do it."

What Nicklaus was doing more than anything else was planning to win. Everyone wants to win. Most golfers—certainly professionals or elite amateurs—intend to win the tournaments they enter. But how many golfers at any level plan to win? Nicklaus did, and it worked for him better than it did any golfer in history as he eclipsed Jones record of 13 majors with 18 of his own—20 if you include his two U.S. Amateur titles—and 19 second place finishes. In fact, of the 80 majors he entered between 1960 and 1980, Nicklaus finished in the top-10 in 65 of them, suggesting that he was able to peak for majors pretty well.

Of course, few golfers at any level can afford to fly to tournament sites weeks before to prepare, or fly to visit their coach or many of the other things that Nicklaus did to make sure his game was at its best for big events. But all golfers can plan their season or year in a way that gives them their best chance of success. There's no option, when you think about it. Failing to plan is planning to fail.

GOAL SETTING

A Harvard University Study showed that 3% of graduating students from the Class of 1953 had written down their career goals. Twenty years later, a team of researchers interviewed students from that class and found the 3% who had written down their goals were worth more financially than the other 97% combined.

Obviously goal setting is a vital step in the planning process. In sports or in life, goals guide our actions and focus our energy, providing a road map to follow. A goal is anything you may wish for or choose to achieve. They are where dreams that come true get their start. They can be long-term, "I want to play on the LPGA Tour" or short-term, "I want to beat my buddies in our putting contest on Friday," but they have to be yours and yours alone. Goals work best when smaller ones provide the foundation for your bigger ones (for example, the extra practice you put in to win those putting contests might help you actually make the PGA Tour). Others can help you reach your goals, or help you understand what your goals are, but choosing them is your job. Goals are like a map, after all, if you don't know where you are going, any road will take you there.

Instead, goal setting allows you to:

- Establish exactly where you want to go.
- Identify the 'roads' that you can take to get there.
- Help you realize when you have arrived.

Engaging in formal goal setting, where you write down your plans in the short and long term and consult with a coach on how you plan to achieve them, can shift good intentions into positive results.

Goals can:

- Help you monitor and improve your performance.
- Improve the quality of your practice and play by replacing boring routines with challenges.
- Replace fear and tension with focus.
- Provide motivation during slumps, injuries and over the course of a long career.
- Reaching your goals helps you develop confidence.

Not all goals are created equally. Everyone with a driver and a single-digit handicap can say their goal is to make the PGA Tour or the LPGA Tour or to play Division I college golf. But saying isn't doing. Setting such a lofty goal is a good thing only if it inspires you to take all the small steps required to become the best golfer you can. That requires you to set SMART GOALS.

What makes a goal a SMART GOAL? After you set a goal such as, "I want to break 70," ask yourself, is it:

- **Specific.** Is this goal clear?
- **Measurable.** Can you objectively prove that you have met this goal?
- **Adjustable.** If you achieve this goal sooner than anticipated, can you increase the intensity of the goal, or does it need to be scaled down to be more realistic?
- **Realistic.** Do you REALLY believe you can do this?

- **Time-based:** Have you set a date by which you and your coach are honestly going to measure that you have met this objective?

An example of a SMART GOAL might be similar to the one stated above (who wouldn't want to break 70?), but differ in some telling ways. Instead of musing about breaking 70 (or 75 or 80) for the first time, a SMART GOAL might be to "Lower my handicap index from 5.0 on June 1 to 2.5 by September 15th."

It's a SMART GOAL because it is:

- **Specific.** It states exactly what you want to achieve
- **Measurable.** It can be calculated easily and objectively.
- **Adjustable.** It can be reset if needed.
- **Realistic.** It is realistic given the current skill level of the golfer (a drop from a 5.0 to a 1.0 might be less realistic) and a commitment to an organized program that includes training, coaching competition and evaluation.
- **Time-based.** It has a definite date.

So you want to set SMART GOALs. But that's just part of the equation, as reaching one major goal likely requires the setting of several other intermediate goals. The process of reaching intermediate goals creates the momentum that makes reaching larger goals possible, while at the same time making the major goals seem less daunting by breaking them down into smaller and more achievable steps.

STEP 1: SETTING YOUR OUTCOME GOALS

These are the goals that you lie in bed thinking about, the ones that get you pumped up: setting a course record, winning a significant tournament or earning that scholarship. When Tiger Woods taped Jack Nicklaus's career records on his bedroom wall, he was setting the mother of all outcome goals: to become the best player in the history of the game. Outcome goals are what you hope to get out of all the work you put in. Setting them is fun. You can set them on a yearly basis or even look beyond that. But outcome goals require a note of caution.

It's essential to set outcome goals, but they need to be kept in their proper place—away from the golf course. Focusing on trying to set a course record after going three under through three holes is about the surest way not to set a course record, and play the next three holes in three over. To play your best, you need to keep your mind clear of 'result' oriented or outcome-based thinking. Set your outcome goals, then file them away leaving your mind clear to focus on the process of achieving them. Great golfers let results happen and trust their preparation to get them where they need to go, playing each shot as an island unto itself.

STEP 2: SETTING THE PHYSICAL PERFORMANCE GOALS NEEDED TO ACHIEVE YOUR OUTCOME GOALS

Practice is important, but goal-setting allows you to practice with purpose, which is even more important. If your outcome goals include lowering your handicap, setting physical goals allows you to figure out how. Some examples:

- Lowering your short-game handicap by a specific number by a specific date. Improving your driving accuracy— setting a target for the percentage of fairways you expect to hit on average in competition this coming season.

- Set a target for the percentage of greens in regulation you expect to hit in competition this coming season.
- Learn a knockdown shot.
- Improve your clubface position at the top of the swing.
- Learn to keep your eyes 'quiet'—focused on the target throughout the stroke.
- Keep your front wrist bowed when chipping.

STEP 3: DEVELOP A STRATEGY TO ACHIEVE EACH STATED PHYSICAL PERFORMANCE GOAL

The goals in step two are only examples of what you may need to work on to reach your outcome goals, but once you've decided the physical aspects of your game you want to improve, you need to figure out how to make that happen. For example, if better bunker play was one of your physical performance goals, a strategy to meet that goal might include a coaching session concentrating on the fundamentals of sand play and making sure your technique and equipment are sound. Next you would plan to practice your bunker play three times a week until you sink five sand shots each session. Each of your physical performance goals requires similar attention to detail, so consult with your coach and get to work.

STEP 4: ESTABLISH YOUR MENTAL PERFORMANCE GOALS AND OUTLINE A STRATEGY TO MEET THEM

While perhaps not as obvious as physical goals, reaching physical goals requires an organized mental approach. Some examples include aiming to:

- Prepare a written game plan with targets for each competitive round.

- Use deep breathing and other relaxation techniques when under pressure.

- Remain positive after poor shots or bad breaks.

- Follow your mental pre-shot routine 90% of the time during a round.

- Complete post-round reports and mental game questionnaires after every round.

- See the target clearly on 80% of all shots in each round.

- Replace mechanics with feel while competing.

STEP 5: BALANCE GOALS

Life doesn't stand still for golf. In fact it's unhealthy and counterproductive to try and make life stand still—"I'll do my homework later, I need to practice if I'm going to make the PGA Tour!"—for golf. In reality, if you let your homework pile up, not only will your school work suffer, but your golf will too, as the stress of poor grades will likely leak into your golf game. Instead, it's much wiser to take the steps necessary to balance the demands of golf and the other realities of your life so that both spheres benefit. Though not as easy to quantify as hitting a certain number of fairways in a round or taking two strokes off your handicap, there are some useful steps you can take to find the right balance between school, golf, family, friends, relationships and personal time.

Consider, for example, that we have about 112 waking hours to 'spend' each week. A good exercise is to calculate how many hours you are in school or doing homework; how many hours you plan to practice, train and play golf and how many hours you expect to devote to family dinners or activities. As you probably are realizing, it doesn't leave much time for video games or simply hanging out with your friends—though there is a place for that. A typical break down for an elite golfer might look like this:

- School and golf—65% of your time, or about 73 hours per week
- Family—10%, or about 11 hours per week
- Friends—10%, or about 11 hours per week
- Personal (reading, television, internet)—10%, or about 11 hours per week
- Relationships—5%, or about 6 hours per week

As you may have gathered by now, if you are serious about becoming the best golfer you can be and competing against players with the same goals, it's not going to happen by accident. There might be a lucky few who reach great heights by talent alone, but only a diligent and goal-oriented approach will allow you to truly reach your potential.

PERIODIZATION

With your goals all nicely planned and laid out, the natural instinct is to spend every possible moment going all out to try and reach them, like, now. As in, yesterday or the day before that. And there is some merit to that approach. Being impatient to succeed is a good quality to have if you really are trying to be your best. But now that you're all pumped up, you need to step back a little bit and do some additional planning. It might be dull, but it's important. Going all out all the time is physically and mentally impossible. Physically, the most likely end result is an acute injury or chronic pain, likely due to over use. Mentally, the most likely outcome is a case of burnout. If you focus all your energy on something all the time and somehow fall short or don't achieve your standards exactly when you'd like, the tendency is to become frustrated or disenchanted. Sometimes you just get bored.

Periodization is a concept designed to help elite athletes avoid just those scenarios. Its origins are in the former Soviet Union where coaches used it as a means to control every detail of the lives or aspiring Olympians. But as it's developed and been adapted for more mainstream use, it's considered an all-inclusive or 'umbrella' plan that helps athletes and coaches chart a path toward peak performance at certain stages of a competitive cycle. At its most comprehensive stage, it includes detailed plans for all aspects of physical workouts, diets, scheduling, training, competition and other considerations. It's common in Olympic-style sports like track and field or rowing but increasingly, its principles have been adopted and adapted for sports like golf, which traditionally have had less structured routines for training and competition.

The overall concept is quite simple. Just like a single practice session includes time for warm-up and preparation and gradually more intense and detailed work before a gradual warm down, your entire season can be planned along the same lines. You can even plan multiple years at a time, creating building blocks that come together to create a more powerful whole. (Olympic athletes plan their training in four-year cycles.)

An 'Annual Plan' (periodized plan) gives you the best chance of performing your best at key times through the year, and proceeding with the confidence that your golf development is modeling the training techniques and principles of the best athletes in all sports.

There are a couple of key points to consider at this stage. One is how many tournaments it's appropriate for you to play in a given season and when you will play them. Another is how you will pay for them. In other words, scheduling and budgeting.

Competing is—or should be—fun, the reward for all your hard effort. But it's unwise to simply enter every tournament you can because they're there. As a high-performance athlete, it's critical to plan your schedule thoroughly, making sure you have the correct blend of preparation, competition and rest—not to mention family, school, friends and the other aspects of a balanced life. Planning your schedule is your responsibility, not your parents or your coaches. Obviously, both need to be consulted, but you need to be the one thinking what is most important to you and what you want to get out of your year. Remember, too many events and you risk not having enough time to keep your skills sharp and your enthusiasm high. Too few events and you risk not being 'tournament ready'—the tension can overwhelm you because you're not used to it, or you can drown in your own enthusiasm because you've been waiting so long to take your skills from the range to the golf course. The right number of events is the one that allows you to prepare properly for competition and yet feel comfortable, rested and confident in a tournament setting.

It's a simple process, but it takes some thought. Take a calendar out and pencil in the events you want or need to play in. Factor in travel, practice and rest. Look at your outcome goals and ask yourself, does this tentative schedule allow you to do what you need to do to meet them? Can you maintain the right balance between golf and your other commitments? Does it allow you to prepare ideally for your 'majors'? Do your parents see it the same way you do? Does your coach? If you can answer all these questions satisfactorily, you probably have a pretty good schedule. Mark it down in pen. If not, rework it until you can.

Now for another dose of reality. Everyone would love to play golf in the best tournaments held at the best courses. We all want the best and latest equipment, the precise coaching we need and the opportunity to travel in style. But it all costs money—usually your parent's money. So before your schedule can be considered final, you should go through the process of budgeting for it. How much are the tournament entry fees for the events you want to enter? What does your club membership cost? How about range balls, shoes and that new driver you want? Hotels for tournaments? Your coaching fees? It all adds up, and before your planning is complete, you should break out the calculator and do exactly that. Is this budget something you and your parents can live with? If so, you are ready to begin planning your season in earnest.

PERIODIZATION IN PRACTICE, A SAMPLE PROGRAM

While programs will vary according to individual needs, for our purposes, let's assume that a 52-week calendar will be divided into four distinct phases, with a goal of 'peaking'—or playing your best golf in May-to-September, the prime tournament season.

PHASE ONE: PRE-COMPETITIVE (JANUARY 1 to APRIL 30)
WEEKS 1 THROUGH 17

This is the time of year when you get yourself and your game in shape for the golf that really counts. Along with your coach, it is during this period that you will:

- Work weekly with a coach on swing technique, mental game skills, rules of golf, strategies and tactics training.
- Complete goal setting.
- Complete your tournament schedule.

- Complete and submit tournament entry forms.

- Make any necessary equipment changes.

- Continue with your fitness regimen, focusing on increasing strength, stamina, and flexibility.

- Review fundamentals—grip, stance, posture, alignment and ball position.

- Prepare a detailed practice plan.

- Start a practice regimen to improve skills in putting, short game, full swing and shot routines.

- Play non-competitive 'discovery' golf, where you test your new skills and find out just where your game is at and how it is progressing.

- Determine exact carry yardages for all clubs.

- Make any special arrangements required to balance school, work and practice.

- Establish a budget to cover equipment, travel, coaching, training and other costs. Build your training and practice intensity over the 17 weeks as advised by your coach so you are ready to compete when the tournament season begins.

**PHASE TWO—COMPETITIVE SEASON (MAY 1 to SEPTEMBER 15)
WEEKS 18 THROUGH 35**

This is the time of year when you realize all those outcome goals you've been working so hard to reach, and when you play your 'majors'—the tournaments that are most important to you, whether it's your club championship, or regional or national tournaments. It's when you want to be at your best and you've planned to make it happen by:

- Working with a coach two or more times per week

- Playing tournaments, trusting your preparation
- Pursuing some other activities to provide a break from golf to help stay fresh
- Continuing your fitness regimen to maintain gains from the pre-season. Develop a pre-set practice regimen that supports your competitive schedule and builds on your pre-season work.
- Staying in regular contact with your coach according to a pre-determined schedule
- Collecting tournament statistics; prepare mental game evaluations; and maintain a USGA handicap
- Doing short-game testing
- Preparing game plans and course maps for each competitive round
- Preparing written mental plans for each round
- Monitoring equipment—grips, lies and lofts
- Reflecting daily on your goals—outcome goals and process goals
- Monitoring your budget
- Maintaining a competitive USGA handicap

PHASE THREE—POST-COMPETITIVE SEASON (SEPTEMBER 16 to OCTOBER 15) WEEKS 36 THROUGH 40

This is the time of year to gather yourself after a long and challenging season of golf. Between training and competing, you've been going hard for nine months. It's time to wind down and relax while focusing on the following:

- Review the season with your coach—evaluate progress versus written goals, give and receive feedback—make plans for the next season.

- Continue your fitness regimen, though at a lighter intensity, perhaps with a focus on cross-training.
- Play for fun with friends and family.
- Reflect and evaluate on your competitive season. What story do your statistics tell you about your game? Do you need to re-focus your goals?
- Make a rough plan for next season.
- Make any necessary technical changes.
- Pursue other interests not related to golf.

PHASE FOUR—OFF-SEASON (OCTOBER 16 to DECEMBER 31) WEEKS 41 THROUGH 52

No matter how much you love golf, you need an off-season, a time when everything else in your busy life can take precedence over golf for once. Mike Weir, the 2003 Masters champion, lives in Draper, Utah when he's not traveling on the PGA Tour precisely so he can get away from the game. He skis with his family and takes fishing trips with his friends. The closest he gets to golf will be standing in front of a mirror for a few minutes each day to check his grip, posture and alignment. It was this relaxed off-season regimen he credits for helping him have the best season of his career when he won the Masters and two other events while finishing fifth on the money list. Naturally many things fell into place that season, but one of the biggest factors he said was that he got away from golf and started the year fresh and enthusiastic. That's what an off-season is for.

It's your time to:

- Recuperate physically, mentally and emotionally.
- Maintain your fitness.

- Focus on school, work and family.
- Cross train, play other sports.
- Take up a new hobby.

And so you have it: Your plan to win.

Becoming an elite golfer is a worthy project, and like all things worthwhile, not something that 'just' happens because someone is 'talented' or 'lucky.' If you are going to make the commitment to be your best—whatever that ends up being—you owe it to yourself to apply these principles so you can be sure you're replacing luck with good planning. Plan to win.

9

THE FACTS ABOUT COLLEGE GOLF

THE STORY OF HOW THE GREATEST GOLFER to ever play at one of the most storied golf programs in the United States goes like this: Jim Weaver, the coach at what was then Wake Forest College, was determined to make the North Carolina school a factor in golf. In particular he wanted to beat nearby Duke University, a hated rival. It was the late 1940s and Duke had qualified to advance in a tournament while Wake Forest had missed the cut. Duke coach Ellis 'Dumpy' Hagler told Weaver, "That's all right, Jim, your guys can caddie for our team."

That was the last straw for Weaver. He decided he was going to recruit a team that would leave Duke in the dust. A year or so later, he had already lined up a promising amateur named Marvin "Buddy" Worsham, who was from a well-known golf family—his brother Lew Worsham was a three-time runner up at the U.S. Open.

But Marvin Worsham wasn't the recruit that changed Wake Forest golf history, at least directly. He did call his new coach and tell him about a big strong kid from Latrobe, Pennsylvania with whom he'd battled in amateur golf. "Well, how good is he?" was Weaver's question. "Coach Jim, he is better than I am," was Worsham's answer.

"Tell him to come on," the old coach replied. "We'll find a nail to hang him on."

The new recruit, who was a nice kid and could hit it a mile, went by the name Arnold Palmer.

This tale of how Palmer made it to Wake Forest, should be required reading for anyone hoping, dreaming and planning to play big-time college golf and eventually, perhaps, play professionally.

From it, you can learn many things. First and perhaps most important, is that recruiting isn't destiny. While college coaches do their best to identify the top talent they can find and make sure they are people of character and commitment, who recruits you, where you end up going and what kind of scholarship you get doesn't necessarily determine your golf future. Golf is a game where your potential isn't fully realized for years, even decades. It's flattering to be recruited by perennial powerhouses that boast multiple NCAA championships and long-lists of All-Americans, but whether you're one of the chosen few to play your college golf there, or if you end up playing at a small but well-respected Division II school with a strong program in the academic area of your choice, your future in golf will still come down to you and your clubs. Palmer might not have been the most high profile golfer recruited to come to Wake Forest during his freshman year, but after a career that included 62 PGA Tour wins and seven majors, he's the highest profile former Wake Forest player, by a country mile.

Another worthwhile point is to consider how college golf has changed in the 50 or so years since Palmer was a Deacon. While Palmer was the catalyst for the development of a remarkable golf tradition there, Wake Forest hasn't won an NCAA championship since 1986 and until Bill Haas joined the PGA Tour as a rookie in

2006, the program hadn't produced a PGA Tour regular since Len Mattiace left in 1990.

This isn't because Wake Forest has suddenly become a poor place to play college golf, or the weather has turned bad in North Carolina. It's because college golf has become terrifically competitive.

"Nowadays, you go to a big junior tournament and there are 100 college golf coaches there," Wake Forest head coach Jerry Haas—brother to PGA and Champions Tour star Jay Haas, and uncle to up-and-coming Bill—said in an interview recently. "Even back in my day (in the early 1980s) you were glad when you got a letter from a golf coach."

This is music to your ears, right? Here is the coach of one of the most respected golf programs in the United States talking about how active the recruiting scene is and how hard it is to get the players he wants. "Where do I sign up?" you're probably thinking.

Well, we'll get to that. But first, the facts.

COLLEGE GOLF: MANY ARE CALLED, FEW ARE CHOSEN

Playing college golf is a worthwhile goal, whether you reach it or not. At the very least, having it as a goal should help you improve your golf game, as making the jump to college golf should provide plenty of motivation for practice and training. And it should help you be aware of your school responsibilities as well, given that you can't play—regardless of your handicap—until you meet the academic requirements. So the worst case senario is that you're a better student and a better golfer than you would be if you didn't set out to play at the Division I level.

At this point, it's worth mentioning that there is more to college golf than the Division I powerhouses that expect to compete for an NCAA title every season. Remember that there are nearly 300 Division I schools. Then there are approximately 200 teams at the Division II and 270 teams at the Division III levels; there are 174 smaller schools that field golf programs in the National Association of Intercollegiate Athletics (NAIA). Another entry point to college golf is the National Junior College Athletic Association with nearly 200 more teams. Sometimes the most important aspect of playing golf at the collegiate level is finding where the best fit for your game and your academic and athletic goals is. In 2008 there were 12,364 male players at all of these schools combined. This offers opportunities for most top class high school players to play somewhere, if they desire.

But it's important to understand what you're trying to do. No one ever successfully climbed Mount Everest by underestimating what it took to get to the summit of the world's tallest mountain. And while playing for Wake Forest or any other college program isn't quite like scaling Everest, it's not a walk in the park either. If you're even considering playing Division I golf, you are likely a very good player; certainly among the best juniors at your club and the best on your high school team. More than likely you are one of the best players in your area and have had some success competing regionally or even further afield. But keep in mind the world of golf is shrinking. Annika Sorenstam arrived at the University of Arizona from Sweden; Luke Donald was recruited from England to play at Northwestern; Adam Scott made it to UNLV from Australia. Elite NCAA recruit worldwide for talent.

So just getting to Division I is a feat in itself. But if your real goal is to get to the PGA Tour, earning the chance to play in college is certainly a key step, but it's hardly a guarantee of success at the professional level. Which isn't to say you shouldn't aim high, only that it's important to see the whole picture when planning a future in golf.

How difficult is it to get a college golf scholarship? Consider some of these numbers:

- There are about 163,341 males who play on high school teams in the United States.
- If you assume a quarter of those are seniors, that means there are about 41,000 males in their last year of high school golf. Since most varsity teams are likely more heavily weighted to seniors than freshman, the real number is probably a little higher.
- There are only about 300 schools that play NCAA Division I men's golf in the United States.
- There are about 3,200 men playing on those Division I teams.
- If you assume about a quarter of those are graduating seniors, that means each year there are roughly 800 openings for freshman across all 300 Division I programs.

Have you done the math yet? If you have, you'll realize why getting the chance to play golf in college is hardly a gimme. There are about 50 high school senior golf team members competing for every available spot in Division I golf. Do you feel confident you would be the favourite to win a tournament against 49 other high school seniors? Of course there are other things you can do to tilt the field in your favor. Excelling academically is one. Being able to manage the requirements of competitive golf and a full course load is not something everyone can do. If you have a proven ability to do that in high school (i.e., a track record of good grades along with an impressive golf resume), college coaches might consider you more favorably than a player with similar golf skills and accomplishments but a spotty academic record. Having a solid character (easy to coach, pleasant to deal with) helps as well, as does your ability to interact positively with a team.

So let's assume you're a good student, a good person and one of the best players for miles around, good enough to get that college scholarship. Surely that means you're a 3-wood and 9-iron away from the PGA Tour? Think again. You want numbers? We have numbers.

- In the 10-year period from 1997 to 2006 only 7 NCAA Division I golfers jumped directly from college golf to the PGA Tour: Tiger Woods, Ryan Moore, J.B. Holmes, Jeff Overton, Anthony Kim, Matt Kuchar, and Matt Davidson.
- In that decade, roughly 8,000 golfers teed it up on the Division I level.
- That means that even the best college-aged golfers in the United States (a population that includes players from all over the world) have a 1-in-1,150 chance of making the PGA Tour directly from their university program.

It's not entirely hopeless. As in anything, persistence can pay off. At the conclusion of each season, the Golf Coaches Association of America (GCAA) recognizes the top performers nationally in NCAA competition. These players are named to the 'All-American Team.' The 'All-Americans' are the 'All-Star Team' of collegiate golf. These players are truly outstanding. They represent about

1% of the total number of NCAA Division I players. And while, as the numbers in the previous section suggest, the odds of making the jump from college golf to the PGA Tour are long. The numbers show the odds are better for All-Americans. As long as they are willing to be patient.

For example, through the end of the 2007 PGA Tour season:

- Of the All-Americans from the 1994 to 2003 period, 33% earned their PGA Tour card at some point.
- 10% of these players have won a PGA Tour event.
- 4% have won multiple times on the PGA Tour: Tiger Woods, Justin Leonard, Ben Curtis, Luke Donald, Rory Sabbatini, Chad Campbell, Heath Slocum and Aaron Oberholser.
- 3% have competed in the Ryder Cup: Tiger Woods, Chris Riley, Justin Leonard, Stewart Cink, JJ Henry and Luke Donald.
- 1.5% of these players (3/2006) have won a professional 'major': Tiger Woods, Ben Curtis, and Justin Leonard.

So there is light at the end of the tunnel. And the PGA Tour and LPGA Tour and all that comes with them are such bright lights that it's hard not to get excited by the prospect. But the 'tunnel' is absolutely crucial, more important than the light itself. While pursuing your dreams of professional golf is noble, the reality of how difficult it is to reach such a lofty goal requires that you make choices that serve not only your golf interests, but your development as a student and a person as well. Spending a decade or more of your life doing everything you can to be the best golfer you can be is a wonderful undertaking, providing that, in the process, you gain a good education, broad life experiences, and you build sound relationships. In that case, when the time comes and you realize that for all your best efforts professional golf is not going to be your path, you can take pride in the journey and make a smooth transition into the next phase of your life.

If you sacrifice your education, life experiences and relationships in the pursuit of golf glory, chances are the transition won't be as smooth and what should be a sense of accomplishment for your efforts will instead be a sense of failure—not only for falling short in golf, but of selling your life outside of golf short in the process.

THE FACTS ABOUT COLLEGE GOLF

ACADEMICS

- Even though golf might be the most important thing in your life, and it's an important factor in deciding what you do with yourself after high school, even a scholarship golf athlete is a student first and athlete second.

- This is as it should be. Studies show that the quality of post-secondary education and training that you receive directly influences the money you will earn in the future, where you will live, who you will marry, the kind of car you will drive and the quality of life you will have. Where you go to college and what you do when you are there is one of the most important decisions you will make in life.

- So find time to prepare properly for your SAT test. Be the athlete that college coaches know they will have few problems with academically, rather than the athlete they hope they will have little problem with academically. There is an art to mastering the SAT, take the steps necessary to understand the process. Consult your guidance counselor or prep information, consider taking courses or consulting books or web-based materials that help those writing the test; write it a second time if necessary.

- Once you get to college and start playing golf, your free time will disappear between practice, travel and academic demands. One solution is to spread your course work over five years.

GETTING RECRUITED

- Don't be shy. Tiger Woods never had a problem getting noticed when it came time to get a golf scholarship, but most golfers aren't in that category. Even if you're a very good player, you have to remember there are a lot of very good players out there. It's up to you to make sure you get noticed. Apart from playing well at key events, this can include creating a resume and cover letter that details your golf background and sending it to the schools that interest you.

- Don't leave it too late—the results of the season heading into your junior year as well as the results from your junior season are highly relevant to golf coaches, and by this time you should have a good idea about which schools might be a good fit for you academically and athletically.

- Don't lie to yourself or potential coaches. If you are a good but not great player based on past results, don't waste your time or anyone else's focusing on going to the University of Georgia or Oklahoma State or one of the other traditional powers. Look at your game, look at your results, consult people close to you and focus on schools that are the right match.

- Don't lie II—it's tempting to dress up your playing resume to look a little shinier than it is, but don't do it. If coaches are serious about you, they will check the information you provide them. The fastest way for them to drop you from consideration is to find out that you exaggerated your results.

- Make sure you know what you are getting into. You are permitted five on-campus visits, paid for by the school, before you decide where to attend. Use those visits to narrow your choices.

- Approach recruiting services with caution. They are expensive and some are better than others. Do your research, talk to those with good and bad stories to tell. Find one that has a proven track record in golf, and be aware that some college coaches don't look favorably on athletes recommended by recruiting services.

- What do recruiting services do? For a flat fee or sometimes a percentage of the scholarship they help find for you, they market your name to coaches and schools that might not automatically be on your radar. This can be helpful, but it's always wise to ask yourself a key question: Why do I need this service?

- Be persistent. You are likely to hear some "no's" before you hear a "yes."

SCHOLARSHIPS

- First, understand what a scholarship really is. It's not free money. It's a grant you receive from the school to offset the financial burden of enrolling there. Just because you get an athletic scholarship, doesn't mean you can't get an academic one too.

- Your scholarship is based on performance on the course and in the classroom. Just because you got one to start at a particular school doesn't mean it can't be revoked if you don't meet certain standards of performance in golf and in academics.

- Don't expect to get a 'full ride.' NCAA Division I men's golf programs have a maximum of 4.5 scholarships to award. NCAA DII programs may have up to 3.5 scholarships to award. NCAA DIII programs do not offer scholarships based on athletic prowess. There are typically eight to 12 players on each team. Even highly regarded freshman are fortunate to get more than 50% scholarships. Some players receive no scholarship money.

- Schools are not permitted to pay your way for visits home at Thanksgiving and Christmas and other times of the year when flights and travel are already expensive. Keep that in mind when mulling over the offer from that school in Hawaii.

- What does this mean? If you're going to school out of state, you may need to pay $10,000 to $20,000 in addition to the scholarship money you receive. It's not uncommon to graduate with an accumulated student debt of $50,000 or more.

- Women's teams have as many as six scholarships to grant because of the equality provisions put in place by Title IX legislation.

- Just because you make the team, doesn't mean you play. Five players usually are included in the 'traveling team' for each tournament. Those spots are awarded by the coach based primarily on team qualifying results. If you don't perform, you're staying home.

- If you do get an offer for a scholarship, make sure you understand every aspect of it. Ask for a detailed written breakdown. Ask questions—how much will you be responsible for and how much will the school be responsible for? Will you need a car at the school? Are there any hidden costs?

GOLF COACHES

- Not all college golf programs are run by coaches who are first and foremost 'swing coaches.' Most college coaches expect their players to arrive on campus with solid games and encourage their recruits to continue their relationship with the coach that got them to the college level.

- College coaches have many responsibilities beyond your golf swing. In fact, you need to take responsibility for your golf swing. College coaches are required to recruit top athletes and plan and execute competitive events while otherwise supporting their athletes.

- If you aspire to be a high-performance golfer, it's your responsibility to have a coaching influence and support team focused on skill development and personal growth.

WHO SHOULD APPLY?

- Outstanding competitive golfers who have a playing resume showing they can qualify for and perform at top events at a 0 handicap level or better.
- Those with solid results: NCAA coaches look at AJGA, USGA and state golf association events that prove you match well with other top golfers.
- Those with sound fundamentals and swing technique; effective practice habits and razor-sharp short games.
- Those with 'Pro' power and ball flight, advanced mental skills and emotional control.
- Solid students with good study habits and a desire to earn a college degree.
- People with good attitudes, strong character and the ability to make the transition from junior golf and high school life to the challenges presented to the collegiate athlete.

FIVE THINGS YOU NEED TO KNOW ABOUT COLLEGE GOLF. NOW.

1. **Be Eligible.** You must meet academic entrance requirements with appropriate SAT scores and a high school transcript that is approved by the NCAA Clearing House. Ask your high school coach or guidance counselor for help if you have any questions.

2. **Be Ready.** The early signing period for high school golfers is in November of your senior year. That means you must be 'scholarship ready' by the end of your junior year. If you are not on a scholarship path by your sophomore year, you are behind.

3. **Be involved** with the right coaches, have a good grasp of the right fundamentals and be a regular at the right tournaments if you want to be someone college coaches come looking for.

4. **Be passionate.** Play because you love the game and you want to explore its limits. Having college golf as a goal should reflect your desire to test your skills against top competition and enrich your college experience.

5. **Be dedicated.** By age 16, golf needs to be your No.1 sport and the one in which you are investing the bulk of your time and energy. That means other sports and activities need to be put aside.

So there you have it. Everything you could ever want to know about what it takes to become the best golfer you've ever dreamed of becoming. How to even become a professional golfer, or at least put yourself on that path.

This book is the product of thousands of hours and decades of teaching, learning, playing, watching, dreaming, talking and writing about golf. This is what some of the most knowledgeable people in the sport know about how to think like an elite player, how to train like an elite player, how to eat like an elite player and how to practice like one, too.

With the right support and the proper dedication, this book can be a guide that will help you become a 'great' golfer.

But that doesn't mean you will play on the PGA Tour or the LPGA Tour. It doesn't mean you will turn professional. It doesn't mean you will play top-flight college golf or even make your high school team.

And it certainly doesn't mean that you should put off the rest of your life just to become a 'great' golfer. Last time we checked, you need to be a student in good standing to be on a high school golf team. And last time we checked, you had to graduate from high school and be eligible for college to play NCAA golf. And…well, you get the picture: It's never just about golf.

And planning to be a professional golfer doesn't mean you don't also have to plan to be a teacher or a doctor or a lawyer or a building contractor. For all but the very few who make it to the highest levels of the game, will need to do something else. If you don't recognize that golf, at least elite golf, eventually ends for almost everyone, then you didn't read this book very closely.

Being a 'great' golfer means being the best player you can become, based on the abilities you have. Because the one thing that 'greats' in almost any field share is a love for what they do. You can't put in the effort required to reach your potential if you don't love what you do. Tiger Woods and Annika Sorenstam have incredible talent, the kind that comes along once in a generation, or even longer. And they have incredible discipline and work habits that allow their talent to shine.

But they have been able to maximize their talent because they love the game of golf. Practice is practice, but if you love the sound, feel and process of the game, it's not a chore, it's an opportunity.

The best way to approach your Journey to Excellence is to understand that it's more about the journey than the excellence and it's more about life than golf.

Put it this way, while working on your putting will have very little impact on your grades, if you take the same step-by-step approach to improving your grades as you do your putting, chances are, they will improve considerably.

And let's say that somehow you don't become an elite golfer. Does that mean spending so much time and energy trying to master a game that defies mastering was poorly spent? No. Far from it. There are no failures in life, only lessons.

If you put everything you can into the game and don't reach all the goals you set for yourself, consider yourself lucky because as long as you did your best you will know that you reached your potential which is something not many people can say about themselves in any field.

And, hopefully, it means you've learned what it takes to be your best at whatever you do, and that's the most important journey anyone can ever take.

ABOUT THE AUTHOR

HENRY BRUNTON is one of the most recognizable names in Canadian golf and is one of the world's leading golf coaches and educators. He is the Royal Canadian Golf Association's National Golf Coach, the creator of the Canadian PGA's Teaching and Coaching Certification program, a CPGA Master Professional, the only Canadian ever recognized as a *GOLF Magazine* Top 100 Teacher and a U.S. Kids Golf Top 50 Kids Teacher. He is also a member of the Titleist Performance Institute's Junior Advisory Board.

A resident of Stouffville, Ontario, Brunton has been a member of the Canadian PGA since 1984. In 2008 the Canadian PGA honored him with its highest standing—Master Professional. He was also named as the fourth Most Influential Person in Canadian Golf in rankings by Canada's *National Post*.

Brunton has a passion for developing elite junior and amateur golfers. He has been Canada's National Coach since the Royal Canadian Golf Association established its Player Development Program in 1999. Teams led by Brunton won the 2001 Four Nations Cup Championship and the 2003 Americas Cup and have competed for Canada around the globe. Brunton coached the Canadian National Men's Team to a Silver Medal finish at the 2006 World Amateur Championship in South Africa.

Brunton has authored the *RCGA Achievement Guide,* a comprehensive manual for high performance players and coaches. In 1999 he was hired by the Canadian PGA to design and develop a national teacher and coach education program. The result was the highly acclaimed Teaching and Coaching Certification Program (TCCP). The TCCP is a mandatory training program for all CPGA Professionals.

Brunton has received considerable professional training from many of the foremost golf educators in the world. A graduate of the University of Ottawa's Physical Education Program, he has studied and participated in select programs in Scotland, Spain, Sweden, the United States and Canada. He is also an accomplished speaker and consultant. In 2008 Brunton was the keynote speaker at the PGA of America Prestigious Teaching and Coaching Summit. He has also presented at golf conferences throughout Canada as well as in Germany, Puerto Rico, Trinidad and Tobago, in the United States for various PGA Sections and at the Better Golf Through Technology Conference at MIT in Cambridge, Massachusetts.

In addition to his work with the Canadian Men's and Junior Boys National teams, Brunton leads "Strive for Excellence," a comprehensive year-round coaching and training program for aspiring high-level junior and collegiate golfers at his home base at Eagles Nest Golf Course near Toronto. The program has been emulated by teachers around the world.

***

MICHAEL GRANGE has covered golf for *The Globe and Mail* since 1998 and is one of Canada's most accomplished sports writers. His work has appeared in *ESPN The Magazine, The New York Times, ROB Magazine, Saturday Night and Toro,* in addition to all of Canada's major golf publications. He won a 2003 National Magazine Award for a feature in *ROB Magazine* about Chum Limited.

He has been the golf analyst for *The Score Magazine* since 2001, providing insights from golf's most prestigious events, including the Masters and the Ryder Cup. Grange ghostwrites Mike Weir's columns which appear regularly in *The Globe* and collaborated previously with Henry Brunton on a series for *The Globe* called "How Low Can You Go," in which an expert instructor (Brunton) teams with a neophyte golfer (Grange) over two summers to see how much difference proper lessons and practice can make. Grange improved his handicap by nearly 20 strokes.

Grange's favourite golf memory is breaking 90—proof that Henry Brunton can teach. He received a Masters in journalism from the University of Western Ontario in 1995 and lives in Toronto, Ontario with his wife Faeron, daughter Avery, son Ellis and two guinea pigs.